KEEPING THE CHURCH SMALL

Small Group Strategies for Growing Churches

Mike Fabarez and Mark R. Kelley, Editors

COMPASS PRESS
ALISO VIEJO, CA

Keeping the Church Small: Small Group Strategies for Growing Churches
Copyright © 2024 by Mike Fabarez and Mark R. Kelley

Published by Compass Press
145 Columbia, Aliso Viejo, CA 92656

All rights reserved. No part of this book may be reproduced in any form without permission in writing from the publisher, except in the case of brief quotations in articles or reviews.

Printed in the United States of America

Edited by Ruth Staggs
Cover Design by Compass Graphics
Layout by Nelson Whitney

Unless otherwise noted, all Scripture quotations are from the ESV Bible (The Holy Bible, English Standard Version), copyright © 2001 by Crossway, a publishing ministry of Good News Publishers.

ISBN: 978-0-9987172-2-7

Compress Press is a department of Compass Bible Institute. It furthers the Institute's objective of preparing men and women for Christian ministry by providing ministerial and theological training resources. More information can be found at www.compassbibleinstitute.org.

TABLE OF CONTENTS

Contributors   5

Introduction   7

1. Small Groups   9
   Keeping the Growing Church Small
   Mike Fabarez

2. Why Your Small Group Needs You   31
   The Crucial Role You Play in Your Small Group
   Ben Blakey

3. A Case for Sermon-Based Small Groups   45
   Maximizing Your Application of God's Word
   John Fabarez

4. Common Pitfalls   61
   How to Solve Small Group Problems
   Mark Kelley

5. Building Trust   81
   Keys to Authentic Relationships
   PJ Berner

6. Holding Each Other Accountable   95
   Pursuing Holiness with Those in Your Small Group
   Mike Elliott

7. *Discipleship in Small Groups*   *111*
   Making Mature Followers of Jesus
   Bruce Blakey

8. *Caring Well for Those in Your Small Group*   *129*
   A Step-By-Step Approach
   Kellen Allen

9. *Praying Together*   *143*
   A Guide for Effective Group Prayer
   Mike Elliott

10. *Closing the Back Door*   *155*
    How You Can Help People Remain Committed to Church
    Hayden Thomas

11. *Small Small Groups*   *167*
    Why Keep Groups "Small"
    Lucas Pace

CONTRIBUTORS

Ben Blakey (M.Div., Southern Baptist Theological Seminary) Lead Pastor of Compass Bible Church, Treasure Valley, ID.

Bruce Blakey (D.Min., The Master's Seminary) Associate Pastor at Compass Bible Church, Huntington Beach, CA.

Hayden Thomas (D.Ed.Min., in process, Midwestern Baptist Theological Seminary) Lead Pastor of Compass Bible Church, Hill Country, TX.

John Fabarez (M.Div., Southern Baptist Theological Seminary) Staff Pastor at Compass Bible Church, Aliso Viejo, CA.

Kellen Allen (M.Div., in process, Southern Baptist Theological Seminary) Staff Pastor at Compass Bible Church, Aliso Viejo, CA.

Lucas Pace (D.Ed.Min., Southern Baptist Theological Seminary) Associate Pastor at Compass Bible Church, Aliso Viejo, CA.

Mark Kelley (Ph.D., Midwestern Baptist Theological Seminary) Provost of Compass Bible Institute and Staff Pastor at Compass Bible Church, Aliso Viejo, CA.

Mike Elliott (Th.M., The Master's Seminary) Lead Pastor of Compass Bible Church, Tustin, CA.

Mike Fabarez (D.Min., Westminster Theological Seminary) Senior Pastor of Compass Bible Church, Aliso Viejo, CA, and President of Compass Bible Institute.

PJ Berner (D.Min., The Master's Seminary) Lead Pastor of Compass Bible Church, Dallas, TX.

INTRODUCTION

I hope this book has found its way into your hands because you have a desire to be used by God to lead a small group, make your small group better, or want God to generate an increased enthusiasm to see small groups promoted in your church. All the contributors to this book are deeply committed to church small groups because they have seen how the Lord uses them in the lives of Christians to become more conformed to the image of Christ. As Christians, we cannot experience a fraction of what God intended for us to experience as a part of his body without regular and thoughtful participation in small groups.

It is our prayer that God will use the following pages to get you excited about the way small groups can enliven a church, draw people into a deeper and more fruitful relationship with Jesus Christ, and heighten people's love and obedience to God's word. I pray you will find wisdom in these pages and deepen your resolve to see healthy small groups established and thrive throughout your congregation. May the Lord encourage you as you prayerfully consider your role in the sort of Christian small groups discussed in this book.

Pastor Mike Fabarez

Chapter 1

SMALL GROUPS

Keeping the Growing Church Small

Mike Fabarez

Christians meeting together in small groups is nothing new. It is as old as the church itself. And it is important to note that the oldest church, the one found in the pages of the Book of Acts was big, really big—and continually growing. Small groups were and are an essential part of God's plan to keep the growing church small.

Many commands of Christ regarding the Christian life cannot possibly be carried out if God's people continue to gather exclusively in the church's largest context. And that is the reason the early church in Jerusalem, which consisted of thousands, needed to split up to meet regularly in small groups. In other words, to put it in modern terms: Sunday attendance is not enough! Meeting together in small groups is as essential for the twenty-first-century church as it was for the first-century church.

If you are not yet part of a church-based small group, it is our hope that in the course of reading this book you will see the indispensable role they serve in the Christian life—and dive in. If you are already involved in a small group, it is our prayer that the following pages will help you learn to make the most of these important gatherings, not only gleaning the unique resources they provide to become more like Christ, but also becoming increasingly more effective in edifying and encouraging your fellow small group participants. And if you happen to be one of those given the responsibility of overseeing a small group, managing its direction and conversation, it is our hope that each chapter will better equip you to skillfully avoid the pitfalls and assist you in maximizing the impact these vital meetings should have on God's people.

A WORD ABOUT GROWING CHURCHES

God intends for his church to grow—both spiritually and numerically. Not only is that the stated goal in the New Testament, but it is certainly the pattern we see in the Book of Acts. Christ told us that the "gates of hell shall not prevail against" his church (Matt 16:18). And gates are only a problem when the church is envisioned as expanding into enemy territory. There is nothing godly or biblical about circling the wagons and celebrating atrophying numbers in the church of Jesus Christ. The church was designed by Jesus and is guaranteed by the Holy Spirit to grow—as new disciple after new disciple bows his knee to the lordship of Christ. This is our "great commission," to be Christ's ambassadors, his fishers of men, always seizing the opportunities to call the people of our generation to repentance and faith.

The Book of Acts records the obedience of those first-century disciples to proclaim the gospel, and page after page reveals the product of the Spirit's gracious work in their evangelism. We read of swelling numbers gathering to worship and to be instructed in the truth, beginning with 120 people in the first chapter of Acts, growing to 3,000 in chapter two, and to 5,000 in chapter four. From there we see phrases like "multitudes," "numbers multiplied," "great numbers," and "increased in numbers" as we continue to read of the growth during the earliest history of the church (5:14; 6:7; 11:21; 16:5).

Of course, not every Bible-teaching evangelical church is currently in a major season of numerical growth, but we should be quick to abandon the all-too-common belief that stagnant or declining church numbers somehow indicate that a church is more godly than one whose attendance is growing. Yes, many heretical churches can boast of incredibly large numbers, just as a professional football team, which has nothing to do with the gospel, can draw tens of thousands to a snowy stadium on a Sunday. But as Spurgeon famously quipped, when it comes to Bible-teaching evangelistic churches, "Those who criticize statistics, are those who have none to report."

It is interesting that often today's churchgoers who seem to revel in their half-empty churches are those who love to quote the likes of Spurgeon, G. Campbell Morgan, R. A. Torrey, D. L. Moody, Martyn Lloyd-Jones, and George Whitefield, when these Bible teachers and the ministries they led were dramatic examples of numerical growth— massive numerical growth! Spurgeon's church sat 5,500 people and in most services, every seat was filled; often people spilled over into a standing crowd of an additional 500. The Chicago Avenue Church, where Torrey and Moody frequently preached, sat 10,000 and was regularly filled to capacity. Historians tell us that Whitefield preached to crowds too large to be accurately counted. The open-air crowds were estimated to be as large as 30,000 people at a time. That is a sea of people, which can only be envisioned by thinking back to the National Mall in DC during a packed presidential inauguration. Like the apostles, these Bible teachers, without the aid of microphones, conditioned their booming voices to loudly instruct the throngs of people who had gathered to hear the word.

Again, such amazing "statistics," as Spurgeon called them, are exceptional in terms of scope and size, but we should pray for and expect an upward numerical trend in our churches, as we seek to be faithful to the call to extend the lordship of Christ, and to teach God's word in our respective corners of Christ's mission field. Growth is not a bad thing; it is a biblical thing. Our concern should be that numerical growth be sought on the basis of uncompromised evangelism, truth boldly proclaimed, and a continual vigilance for maintaining sound doctrine.

THE NEED FOR SMALL

Regardless of the current rate of numerical growth in your church, its size is probably already at a place that makes much of the New Testament's instructions impossible to live out in the context of the whole assembly. Even if your church averages a Sunday attendance of seventy-five to a hundred people, it is hard to imagine how the average Christian could succeed in responding to this straightforward command of Scripture:

> And let us consider how to stir up one another to love and good

works, not neglecting to meet together, as is the habit of some, but encouraging one another, and all the more as you see the Day drawing near. (Heb. 10:24–25)

You may have heard pastors use this passage to exhort Christians to attend the Sunday services, but if you ponder the activities described in the first part of the sentence, you will quickly recognize that the context for this kind of "meeting together" is difficult to imagine in the largest church gathering. If we are to meaningfully stir one another up to love and good works, it can hardly be effectively accomplished when we are sitting next to other Christians in a worship service, worshipping and being taught the word. The "meeting together" in view here is the kind of meeting where everyone has the opportunity to talk, discuss, encourage, follow up, ask questions, be accountable, pray, and share prayer requests. That is, it is a smaller context—a small group.

And that is just one example of the New Testament "one anothers." Consider our call to "love one another" (John 13:34), to "honor one another" (Rom. 12:10), to "welcome one another" (Rom. 15:7), to "bear one another's burdens" (Gal. 6:2), to "instruct one another" (Rom. 15:14), to "submit to one another" (Eph. 5:21), and to "serve one another" (Gal. 5:13), just to name a few of the many New Testament directives.

We may have some of these in view as we interact with people on the church patio after a service, but to measurably accomplish these directives in the lives of other Christians on a regular basis, a secondary context for gathering in the church is a must. The second-century church easily recognized this and embedded the call to multiple meetings and gatherings in their writings. The *Didache*, an early church document summarizing the "teaching of the twelve" states: "You shall frequently gather together, seeing the things that are profitable for your souls" (16:2). The Letter of Barnabas exhorted his readers to "Seek out every day the presence of other Christians" (19:10). The Letter of Ignatius to the Ephesians states, "Be careful to come together often... Assemble frequently" (13:1).

But we don't have to move beyond the New Testament books to feel this fundamental obligation. All we have to do is consider the familiar New Testament word commonly translated as fellowship.

KOINONIA

The word fellowship translates the Greek word *koinonia* and means, "to share together" or "have a common participation."[1] The word fellowship is used both in a passive and an active sense in the New Testament. In a passive sense, the word describes the experience we *share* as Christians ("shared experience"). In an active sense, the word describes the *sharing* we Christians do as a part of God's family ("sharing ourselves").

Let's picture these two distinct aspects of participation with the Christians in our church like this: 1) our lives lived "side-by-side" (passive fellowship) and 2) our lives engaging "face-to-face" (active fellowship). Both play an important role in what the Bible means by our fellowship with other Christians. God designed and directs us to participate in both. And both of these aspects are lived out in, and as an extension of, our small group relationships. Let's first think through the "passive" aspects of fellowship as they impact the "active" fellowship with one another in small groups—which is the focus of this book.

THE "SHARED EXPERIENCE" OF "BIG CHURCH"

The most fruitful small groups begin with the shared experience of attending the same church, sitting under the same teaching, and functioning under the leadership of the same pastors. While many small group models encourage the participation of Christians from a variety of churches, this is not the New Testament pattern, and it also presents the group participants with a variety of counterproductive complications.

Consider, for instance, the problem of a new Christian engaging in a discussion about water baptism amid a conversation regarding the application of a passage in the Book of Acts. The Presbyterians and the Baptists in such a diverse group will have an irresolvable conflict in trying to counsel and direct this young Christian. Or imagine a discussion in 1 Corinthians about church discipline. This varied team of Christians will be hopelessly deadlocked because of the assorted practices and policies of the representative churches within the small group. Practices and understandings regarding the Lord's Supper, the question of women pastors, and the issue of the continuation or cessation of the supernatural gifts will all yield the same kind of frustration. Small groups with participants from several churches, all seeking to engage in this level of biblical fellowship, will always be forced to reduce the discussion and application to the lowest common denominator, and that may lead to avoiding very important topics altogether.

In the New Testament we are told that doctrinal disputes and debated theological practices within a particular congregation are to be deferred to the church's pastors (i.e., overseers, shepherds, elders). These leaders are clearly charged with the responsibility of coming to conclusions on these critical matters and are commissioned to seek unity within their assemblies. Paul writes to the church in Corinth charging, "by the name of our Lord Jesus Christ, that all of you agree, and that there be no divisions among you, but that you be united in the same mind and the same judgment" (1 Cor. 1:10). While all Bible-teaching churches should seek to find agreement regarding the gospel, as well as the person and work of Christ, each local assembly should strive to find agreement in all their important doctrinal assertions and theological practices.

Given the technological age in which we live, I should further add that the "shared experience" of attending the same church should be a physical reality and not a virtual one. Of course, all the ways to digitally eavesdrop on a service or review a recorded sermon are helpful ways to supplement our church involvement, but they should not replace our church attendance. I hope we can all easily attest to the fact that the physical reality of being present and actively involved in a church service has a superior effect not only on our own experience, but also on our fellow brothers and sisters in attendance. So let churches continue to provide these great technological options for those who are sick, shut-in, traveling, or for purposes of review, but as frequently as possible, let us be physically, spiritually, and mentally present for the shared experience of our church's weekly worship service. And let us appreciate the importance of being part of a small group that is united under the theological convictions and biblical values of the same church family.

THE "SHARED EXPERIENCE" IN SERVING

The impact and effect of our small group participation will be enhanced by the *koinonia* of serving in ministry together. The shared experience of "striving side-by-side for the faith of the gospel" (Phil. 1:27) has the effect of welding our lives together as a unified and relationally close team. Obviously, there are few opportunities throughout the year for the *entire* church congregation to serve together in some particular ministry, but this biblical practice is ideal and easily accomplished for the small group or a few individuals from a small group. When Christians from the same small group team up to teach in a children's Sunday School class, work together in the church's evangelistic outreach, help on the hospitality crew, or serve together in the visitation ministry of the church, it has a natural unifying effect.

Paul utilized a vivid Greek word to describe one of his ministry partners. It is a word sometimes translated as "companion," "partner," or "comrade." Older translations often leave in the agrarian image, translating it "yokefellow" or "yokemate." This analogy is easily lost on modern readers. However, one text in which the illustration is often explained by teachers and pastors is in 2 Corinthians 6 where Paul wrote, "Do not be unequally yoked with unbelievers" (v. 14). The "yoke" in this reference, as you'll likely recall, is a large wooden crosspiece laid over the neck of a pair of oxen and attached to the plow for the service of the farmer. That picture of two sturdy oxen linked together and pulling for a common goal is the way Paul described his ministry coworker.

When small group participants enlist in ministries as co-laborers and fellow workers, they are investing not only in ministry but also in an enhanced and more fruitful small group experience. When a relational breakdown between two Christian women, Euodia and Syntyche, occurred in the church at Philippi, the Apostle Paul sought to get these believers to recall their shared experience in serving as "yoked up" co-laborers. Paul's instruction to repair the conflict was for these two ladies to give thought to their past experience in "laboring side-by-side" with Paul and their "fellow worker" Clement (Phil. 4:3). The experiences of sharing ministry goals and expending energy together in the trenches of Christ's work are an important type of *koinonia*, which should tie us together in strong and lasting biblical relationships.

If you are not regularly involved in a ministry at your church, take time to discover what service for Christ your fellow small group participants are currently involved in; then decide to team up with one or two of them and watch what this will do to deepen your relationships. The byproduct of a unified and enriched small group is sure to follow.

THE "SHARED EXPERIENCE" IN REFRESHMENT

Jesus and the apostles were tired and physically drained after ministering to the crowds for hours on end. Jesus said to them, "Come away by yourselves to a desolate place and rest a while" (Mark 6:31). Mark recorded that they had "had no leisure" time and so "they went away in the boat to a desolate place by themselves" (vv. 31–32).

Surely this was not a unique episode in their lives and ministry. They certainly needed regular intervals of "leisure time" to be refreshed and recharged. What is interesting, unlike so many of us today, is Jesus and his apostles frequently did this recharging together. We find the same pattern in the book of Acts, as the early disciples gathered "together with gladness," not only in the context of worship or ministry, but also during those in between times—connecting with one another in homes and over meals (Acts 2:46).

As we can all attest, when we spend times of refreshment together with our brothers and sisters in Christ, it helps to naturally move us from acquaintances to "friends." We could all retreat to our own biological families for our downtime (which is an undeniably important time to schedule and guard), but we also need to schedule some hours of refreshment to just "hang out" with those we will later pray with, serve with, and seek to spiritually encourage.

For most of us, this time needs to be intentional. It will not schedule itself. So, from time to time, before we head off to a sporting event, go shopping, fishing, or play a round of golf, let's make a point to call up someone in our small group and engage in those activities together. We will find that our future small group discussions will be augmented by better and more genuine relationships with those in our group.

ACTIVE KOINONIA

Sharing our experiences in recreation, ministry, and worship is very important. But in each of these situations, our lives with fellow Christians are being lived out side-by-side. While this has the effect of drawing and tying our lives together, these are still only acts of "passive" *koinonia*. However, it is when our chairs turn face-to-face that we begin to engage in the all-important work of "active" *koinonia*. This will feel like a much more vulnerable experience because it will involve a greater degree of personal disclosure, openness, and effort. But these are the kinds of activities that will yield the most important fruits of biblical fellowship and spiritual growth.

Just about all of what goes on in the kind of small groups we will describe in this book will fall into this category of "active" *koinonia*. In the following chapters, we will cover how to set up, guide, and direct these kinds of small group meetings. But for now, allow me to describe the general components of active *koinonia* observed in the Bible, some of which will take place during our weekly small group meetings, and all of which should be intentionally planned.

THE "SHARING OF YOURSELF" BY SHARING YOUR HOME

Small groups are often best conducted in one of the participant's homes. This is the context for much of the *koinonia* we see in the New Testament. In Acts 2, the thousands of congregants in the early church not only met regularly in the public areas of the temple complex, but they were also described as meeting in small groups "in their homes" (v. 46).

Opening our homes for the gathering of Christians should not only be done for small group meetings, it should also become a part of our regular habit as Christians. The word translated "hospitality" in the New Testament gives us a vivid picture of why our "brothers and sisters" should be invited to our homes. The word in the original language of the Greek New Testament is the compound word: *philoxenia*. Perhaps you already recognize the component parts. *Philo* is the Greek root that shows up in the first half of the word "philanthropy." If you've been around church for a while, you've undoubtedly heard the word phileo presented as one of the Greek words that translates into our word for "love." *Phileo* is often described as the familial love of siblings, or "brotherly love." We find the second component, *xenia*, in English words like "xenophobia" which depicts someone who is "afraid" of "foreigners." *Xenos* means "outsider," "stranger," or "foreigner."

When we combine these word meanings with the idea that God has called us as Christians to treat those who share a common commitment to Christ like "brothers and sisters," it makes sense that the word *philoxenia* perfectly applies to our understanding of the idea of hospitality. Our homes are "our" domains. It is expected that they are fully open to our biological families. The people of our church are, naturally speaking, an eclectic group of "outsiders." But the Bible states that now in Christ, they are in fact spiritually connected to us as brothers and sisters through their new birth in Christ. We are a spiritual family. The command for us to have "brotherly love" for them reminds us that these former "outsiders" are to be loved, honored, and accepted as though they were our biological siblings, and that they should now be "invited in"—even to our homes.

That may seem like a roundabout way to discuss the call to open up our homes to our spiritual siblings from church, but the image is rich as it communicates how our "homes" are to be places open to Christians, because of our Christlike "brotherly love" for those who we would have previously considered "outsiders" or "foreigners" to our families. We don't need a Greek New Testament to read a passage like the following one and see how all the elements of *phileo* love change the way we honor and care for our fellow saints:

> Love one another with brotherly affection. Outdo one another in showing honor. Do not be slothful in zeal, be fervent in spirit, serve the Lord. Rejoice in hope, be patient in tribulation, be constant in prayer. Contribute to the needs of the saints and seek to show hospitality. (Rom. 12:10–13)

So then, let's make it our habit, and a consistent practice of our Christian lives to have our homes frequented by those who would not "naturally" be seen there.

THE "SHARING OF YOURSELF" BY SHARING YOUR PRAYERS

It is common to read of the importance of prayer in our Bibles, but it is essential to recognize that a lot of the discussion of prayer in the Scriptures is not the picture of an isolated Christian in his inner room praying to God in secret. Yes, that is a foundational Christian discipline (Matt. 6:6), but often the Bible calls us to pray together, not only in church services, but also in small groups.

Think back to the pattern of Christ, praying not only by himself in solitary places (Mark 1:35), but also desperately wanting Peter, James, and John to fight off their fatigue and to pray together for the trial at hand in Gethsemane (Matt. 26:37–45). Surely there were many times

Jesus prayed in small group settings with his disciples. And this kind of small group praying certainly became the pattern of the early church. In Acts 12, when the church was concerned about Peter's imprisonment, several gathered as a group in John-Mark's childhood home to pray for Peter's release (v. 12). James wrote to tell his readers to "confess their sins to one another and pray for one another" (5:16). Just think of how important it is that small groups of Christians pray for one another as they share their lives, their temptations, their victories, and their struggles. We need to support each other in our Christian lives, and there are few things more necessary than lifting one another up in prayer.

Our weekly small group meetings should certainly include a scheduled time of sharing and praying for one another, but our practice of prayer should go far beyond that. We should be frequently sharing our prayer requests with other Christians and stopping at the slightest provocation to begin to pray together—in the lobby of the church, as we are about to wrap up a phone conversation, in our living rooms, at the coffee shop, or as we drive down the freeway together. Prayer should become a much more frequent part of our time together with other Christians. It has a distinct way of bringing us together in unity, worship, and a common spiritual purpose.

Certainly, the promise of having God's attention in our praying should be enough to motivate much more prayer time, both individually and in groups. Consider the following verses and the amazing promises granted to us in God's word:

Trust in him at all times, O people; pour out your heart before him; God is a refuge for us. (Ps. 62:8)

The LORD is near to all who call on him, to all who call on him in truth. (Ps. 145:18)

If you then, who are evil, know how to give good gifts to your children, how much more will your Father who is in heaven give good things to those who ask him! (Matt. 7:11)

And I tell you, ask, and it will be given to you; seek, and you will find; knock, and it will be opened to you. For everyone who asks receives, and the one who seeks finds, and to the one who knocks it will be opened. (Luke 11:9–10)

For there is no distinction between Jew and Greek; for the same Lord is Lord of all, bestowing his riches on all who call on him. (Rom. 10:12)

Let us then with confidence draw near to the throne of grace, that we may receive mercy and find grace to help in time of need. (Heb. 4:16)

Until now you have asked nothing in my name. Ask, and you will receive, that your joy may be full. (John 16:24)

We have so many needs in our lives, which the Bible says can be dramatically affected by our praying; but sadly, far too often, we miss out on this powerful resource and essential component of biblical fellowship. May we learn to leverage the privilege of praying together, increase the amount of time we spend pouring out our hearts to the Lord, and subsequently watch him work. And let's not forget another benefit of joining together in prayer with other Christians. Paul reminded the Corinthians that as the private prayer concerns of one person became known and prayed for among more of the brothers and sisters in Christ, the thanksgiving and praise to God when he answered were also exponentially increased (2 Cor. 1:11).

THE "SHARING OF YOURSELF" BY SHARING YOUR KNOWLEDGE OF CHRIST

As uncomfortable as it may feel, in one way or another, every Christian is called to be a teacher. Of course, the kind of "teacher" James is warning in James 3:1 is reserved for a select few—a fraternity that should not be eagerly sought, he tells us. But when it comes to the kind of Hebrews 10:24–25 "stirring up" and "encouraging" of one another, every Christian is called to participate. This is the kind of "mutual instruction" Paul expected in every healthy church (Rom. 15:14). Small groups are the perfect setting for this kind of mutual support and instructive encouragement.

As we will later describe in this book, we believe that the discussion and application of the most recent Sunday sermon is the ideal diet for church-based small groups. Though no new biblical teaching or lesson is presented in this type of small group, a discussion that seeks to implement, clarify, and motivate the application of the previous sermon from the main Sunday service will relay plenty of biblical insight and scriptural wisdom. And that can only happen when the participants in a small group bring their growing knowledge of God's word to the conversation.

Instead of sitting around and asking, "What does this passage mean to you?" (which, sadly, is far too common these days), the small groups recommended in this book would advise you to gather to consider the various aspects of appropriate biblical application from a recent sermon that has been carefully exposited. Keeping application appropriate and biblical necessitates biblical knowledge and wisdom, as well as life experience. And in that kind of discussion, each participant is a teacher of sorts.

Unfortunately, the writer of Hebrews was concerned that his readers were incapable of all but the most basic mutual instruction and counsel. Notice his apprehension when after bringing up the Old Testament character, Melchizedek, he says this:

> About this we have much to say, and it is hard to explain, since you have become dull of hearing. For though by this time you ought to be teachers, you need someone to teach you again the basic principles of the oracles of God. You need milk, not solid food, for everyone who lives on milk is unskilled in the word of righteousness, since he is a child. But solid food is for the mature, for those who have their powers of discernment trained by constant practice to distinguish good from evil. Therefore let us leave the elementary doctrine of Christ and go on to maturity, not laying again a foundation of repentance from dead works and of faith toward God, and of instruction about washings, the laying on of hands, the resurrection of the dead, and eternal judgment. (Heb. 5:11–6:2)

This is a stinging indictment for those whose spiritual growth consists of a constant revisiting of their favorite eight or nine Bible verses, and a perpetual rehearsal of the basics of Christian doctrine. We must continue to grow in our knowledge of God's word and its application, so that we may be useful to God and aptly encourage, motivate, and help our brothers and sisters in Christ. Instead of receiving the criticism from the writer of Hebrews, may it be said of us what Paul said of the Christians in the first-century church in Rome: "I myself am satisfied about you, my brothers, that you yourselves are full of goodness, filled with all knowledge and able to instruct one another" (Rom. 15:14).

THE "SHARING OF YOURSELF" BY SHARING YOUR MEALS

Lastly, let me prompt a practice that is so commonplace in the Bible that many fail to note its importance—namely, the practice of God's people sharing meals together. While it may not be possible or practical for a weekly small group discussion to begin with a meal, sharing a breakfast, lunch, or dinner with a couple of our small group participants should be a frequent practice. Recall again that helpful description of the early church in Acts 2, in which we read that the church participants made it their practice to break "bread from house to house, taking their meals together with gladness and sincerity of heart" (v. 46). Perhaps this was so common because the early church had seen and heard how Jesus frequently took his meals not only with his disciples (Mark 6:31), but also with those he was teaching (Luke 24:30), as well as with those he was working to evangelize (Mark 2:16)—sometimes with as many as five thousand people at a time (Mark 6:44),

We can all identify with how sharing a meal breaks down barriers, opens up conversation, and connects people in meaningful ways. Gathering with a small number of brothers and sisters in Christ to share a meal is one of the easiest ways to engage in "face-to-face" active koinonia, which has the inexplicable effect of unifying and enriching our relationships with other Christians. Since we are all already in the practice of eating every day, this common biblical practice of taking our meals together simply involves a shift in our schedule and a purposeful intention. Even right now, it would be easy to stop reading and to pick up the phone to invite one or two of our small group participants to join us for a meal sometime this week.

GETTING TO WORK

When we think through our participation in small groups against the backdrop of the biblical pattern of passive (side-by-side) and active (face-to-face) koinonia, we can see how much of God's call to fellowship takes place within, and as an extension of, the biblical practice of meeting regularly in small groups.

Your reaction to this quick overview may be that it will require way too much of your time. You may be thinking, "I certainly don't have time for all of that." As others have rightly said, "If you are too busy for an essential Christian practice, you're too busy!" Don't gloss over that sentence. It may be that you are in fact too busy. Your meaningful connection with other Christians is not extracurricular—it is very near the center of what it means to be a Christian.

For most Christians, it is not that they are too busy; it is just that their priorities are out of whack. Remember that every Christian has exactly the same amount of time, 168 hours a week. Admittedly we all have to spend about a third of those hours sleeping, eating, and maintaining our hygiene. And for most of us, another third is tied up in earning a paycheck and commuting to the place where we are called to earn that paycheck. But when we add it up, that leaves the average person another third, about fifty or more hours, to spend as he or she chooses. The problem for most of us modern Christians is that we reflect far too many of the patterns of the modern non-Christians—who waste most of that third surfing the internet and watching television.

We all have the call from our Lord to engage with other Christians between Sundays. It should become our top priority to take some of those fifty hours and reallocate them to invest in God's people. I know it is more work than hanging out on the sofa with a laptop or a TV remote, but I hope we will all come to know that investing in God's priorities—in this case, participating in small groups and engaging in fellowship with God's people—will most definitely be worth the effort.

Chapter 2

WHY YOUR SMALL GROUP NEEDS YOU

The Crucial Role You Play in Your Small Group

Ben Blakey

Paralysis is a big problem.

If you stop for a moment to consider the plight of the quadriplegic person, you will be stunned to realize how many basic physical activities you take entirely for granted. From getting out of bed in the morning to brushing your teeth at night, you would be confronted with a myriad of seemingly simple tasks that can no longer be completed without assistance. And virtually no paralysis comes without consequence. Even if you lost the use of only one of your appendages, you would find yourself very limited and handicapped because the body was designed to use all of its parts.

Unfortunately, many churches are suffering from a form of parochial paralysis. The consumerism of our culture has infiltrated the church, and too many people who would consider themselves a part of the body do little or nothing to serve the church. This trend is having a negative effect on all kinds of ministries and churches because the church body was designed to use all of its parts.

In particular, too many small groups experience some kind of paralysis. A good small group must have more than a healthy leader—it must have a healthy body where each member is fulfilling his or her role. That is why this chapter is turning the attention to the small group participant and laying a foundation for subsequent chapters to build upon. Just like the human body or Christ's church, a small group is designed to use all of its parts.

YOUR ROLE IS IMPORTANT

Nobody wants to be underappreciated. It's just about every employee's nightmare to be "overworked, underpaid, and underappreciated." Unfortunately, many small group participants are underappreciating themselves by buying into the subtle lie of, "I'm not the leader of the group, so my involvement isn't really that important, right?"

Wrong.

Each part of the small group is essential, and the whole group will suffer if each part is not doing its job. Again, remember the consequences you would face if your arms or legs decided to take the day off. Now think of the harm that will be done to your small group if its members do not fulfill their roles.

This comparison of the church to a body is nothing new; it goes all the way back to God himself in the inspired pages of Scripture. Along with this analogy comes the truth that each part of the body is indispensable. Consider 1 Corinthians 12:14–15, which says, "For the body does not consist of one member but of many. If the foot should say, 'Because I am not a hand, I do not belong to the body,' that would not make it any less a part of the body." Passages like this (or Rom. 12:4–5) surely stand as a rebuke to anyone who thinks, "Because I'm not the leader I must not be important." Yes, the leader and the participant may have different roles to play, but each part is essential.

The church was never designed to be an organization run by a committed few. The maxim that 20% of the people do 80% of the work may unfortunately be experientially true, but it is not biblical! Many look at their small group leaders or pastors and think, "They are supposed to be doing the work of the ministry, not me!" But this perspective is surely wrong. In fact, the Bible makes it very clear that pastors are supposed to "equip the saints for the ministry" (Eph. 4:12). The pastor's job is not to do the work of the ministry—it's to train you to do that very work. The church, or a small group, will only be healthy when each part is doing its job. Ephesians also reminds us that only "when each part is working properly" will "the body grow so that it builds itself up in love" (Eph. 4:16).

If you are a small group participant, and if you are thinking of your role as inconsequential, you are not merely doing a disservice to yourself—you are handicapping your entire small group. Your group will only be fully healthy when everyone including you is doing their part. Embrace the teaching of the Bible on the importance of the entire church and resolve to fulfill your role with eagerness.

YOU'RE STILL NOT THE LEADER

Perhaps if the Apostle Paul were alive today, he would use a football team to further illustrate the truths expressed by the body analogy in 1 Corinthians 12. Consider for a moment the offensive unit of a football team—what a beautiful picture of teamwork. Here you have eleven men playing very different roles (from blocking, to passing, to receiving the pass) for one common purpose—advancing the ball. If one of these eleven men decides to sit out for a play, the team will have big problems. Every player is important!

Now consider, if instead of being tempted to sit out a play, all eleven men decide they want to be the quarterback on the same play. The problems that ensue would be devastating to the offensive efforts of the team (even if extremely hilarious to any spectators of the game). Having too many quarterbacks on the field, just like too many chefs in the kitchen, is counterproductive. Likewise, your small group will experience trouble if all the members think of themselves as the "leader."

For most small group participants, their job is not to *be* the leader, it is to *follow* the leader. Thankfully, God gives us valuable instructions on how to do this. Hebrews 13:17 says, "Obey your leaders and submit to them, for they are keeping watch over your souls, as those who will have to give an account. Let them do this with joy and not with groaning, for that would be of no advantage to you."

While this verse speaks mainly about pastors/elders, there are several things we can learn here that apply to a small group setting. First, we need to remember that *leaders exist for a purpose*. Church leaders are there to keep watch over your souls. This is an incredibly great and sacred charge that God gives to pastors. God has entrusted them with something so precious it could not even be bought with gold or silver, but only with *the precious blood of his own Son*. What a weighty responsibility! Therefore, pastors throughout the history of the church have realized the necessity of developing undershepherds to help in this careful watch over God's flock. In many churches, small group leaders play an important role in helping pastors keep watch over the people God has entrusted to them.

Second, we learn from Hebrews 13:17 that each member of the church has been charged *to make their leader's job a joy*. A good small group leader will, like your pastors, take a vested interest in your spiritual health. Your actions, therefore, have the potential to cause great joy or grief to your leader. If you are participating in the group and showing clear signs of spiritual growth, your leader is going to be rejoicing over the work of God in your life! On the other hand, if your actions are obviously straying from God's revealed will, you will no doubt cause your leader a great deal of spiritual grief.

Third, the book of Hebrews reminds us that following our spiritual leaders is *for our own good*. The writer clearly tells us that being a source of grief to our leader "would be of no benefit to [us]." Following the lead of your small group leader will not only benefit your group, it will benefit you.

So, what does following your leader look like? Hebrews 13:17 pulls no punches as it commands obedience and submission. While these may not be popular ideas in our individualistic society, you must remember that these directives from God are for your good. If your small group leader is doing their job well, they will simply be helping you apply the

Bible. They will be encouraging you to do things like evangelism and Bible reading. They will be directing you to love your spouse, serve the church, and pursue the Lord. You should obey all these instructions with eagerness.

Submission is also an important part of the small group participant's role. You should always treat your small group leader with grace and respect. It is not your role to be the group contrarian who always seeks to balance, soften, or counter what your leader says. Of course, you may have questions or concerns about something he or she says, but always take care to express this in a way that is respectful and submissive, not subversive.

SO WHAT EXACTLY IS MY ROLE?

In order to understand the role of the small group participant, we must move from explaining what that role is not, to describing what it actually is. Consider this job description:

My job is to actively use my spiritual gifts to support the small-group leader and work toward the benefit of the entire group.

By necessity, this job description is still somewhat vague. Every small group is different, so the roles will vary. Not only this, but every person is unique and brings his or her skills, abilities, and spiritual gifts to the small group table. As the Scriptural "body" analogy has reminded us, we are not all hands or feet or eyes. We have diverse gifts for diverse roles.

We are going to put some meat on the bones of our somewhat

skeletal definition in a moment, but let's first take note of one specific word from our job description: actively. If we are looking for a passive small group role, we'd best get used to disappointment. As we continue to describe the role of the small group participant, every aspect of that role is going to involve *activity*, not *passivity*.

In addition to the small group participant job description, consider these four action words that will help you understand your role.

Prioritize

If the small group leader is the only one who is making the group a priority, the group is destined for failure. Every single member of the group needs to make attendance and participation a priority. Small groups will only succeed when everyone—not just the leader—takes ownership of the group.

Consider for a moment the difference between how you treat your home and how you treated the last hotel room you stayed in. I would be willing to guess that you take much better care of your home. Why? Because you have literally taken ownership of your home! Even if you are a renter, you still have a vested interest in the dwelling place because when tomorrow comes, you will still be the one living there.

Now I doubt that you trashed your last hotel room, but I also doubt that you made the bed before you left. You probably didn't clean the bathroom or take out the trash before checking out, either. Once you leave the hotel, that room is no longer your problem.

Unfortunately, too many people think of their small group as a hotel room, not a home. They are not vigilant in how they think about their group because they think it's someone else's problem. They think their failure to attend or to show up prepared will not affect anyone else. Nothing could be further from the truth.

If you are a participant in a small group, you need to take ownership of your group. No, this does not mean you wrestle control away from your leader—it means you take a vested interest in your group. You need to have a sense of responsibility toward your group and not shirk off the issues there as "someone else's problem."

If you do not feel like you can make your small group a priority, something needs to change. If this group is the main source of fellowship and accountability in your life, clear out your schedule in order to invest the time you need in your group. If you are in several small groups, maybe you should consider cutting back to focus on quality—not just quantity.

Not only do you need to prioritize the group and its meetings, but you also need to prioritize the people in the group. Philippians 2:3–4 says it so clearly, "Do nothing from selfish ambition or conceit, but in humility count others more significant than yourselves. Let each of you look not only to his own interests, but also to the interests of others."

As you are walking into your small group, you need to bring the mindset that everybody else there is more important than you. To borrow from one American President, ask not what your small group can do for you—ask what you can do for your small group. If the small group leader is the only one thinking this way, you have a handicapped small group. Make sure you are doing your part to prioritize your small group and the people in it.

Prepare

If you are like me, your heart dropped every time you heard a teacher say the words "group assignment" in class. I would always have this unsettled feeling that the project would be "group" in name only and that I would end up doing most of the work myself. While part of that may have been my fault, I had experienced too many group assignments where it felt like I was the only one to show up prepared.

I wonder how many small group leaders feel this way every week. They have thoughtfully and prayerfully gone over the material, but they walk in with this unsettled feeling that no one else has. If you are a small group participant, do your best to change that.

Many church small groups will have some kind of homework—questions to answer or material to read. One of the simplest and clearest responsibilities you have as a small group member is to do that homework. Show up prepared!

Another crucial element of small group preparation is that of prayer. As we like to say at Compass Bible Church, "Pray up before you show up." Both Scripture and church history pound home the importance of prayer in preparation. What did Jesus do before he chose his disciples? He spent the whole night in prayer (Luke 6:12). How did Martin Luther feel when his schedule was overflowing? He famously said, "I have so much to do that I shall spend the first three hours in prayer." Surely spending time in prayer before attending small group is a good investment.

The possibilities for a pre-small group prayer list are endless: pray through the homework or the topic at hand, ask God that it would be an effective time, pray for your leader as he or she guides the conversation, pray for each person in your small group and ask that the meeting would benefit them.

While there is no shortage of prayer requests, there is often an unfortunate shortage of prayer, which again leads to handicapped small groups. Remember that apart from Christ, you (and your small group) can do nothing, so ask him for help. Pray up before you show up.

Participate

At the time of this writing, my wife and I are new parents. God blessed us with a wonderful little girl named Hannah. We love spending time with her and enjoy seeing the new facial expressions she makes as she learns to smile and use the muscles God has designed for her. But at this point, conversations with Hannah don't get very far. You can try saying as much as you want to her, but she is not going to say anything back to you. If you're lucky, you may get a quick giggle, and if you're not, she'll cry. But she is not going to say anything coherent, so your conversational efforts aren't going to get anywhere.

One-sided conversations just don't work, and neither do one-sided small groups. Unfortunately, I fear that many small group leaders feel like they are trying to have a conversation with my daughter—and they're getting nowhere. Small groups will be handicapped unless each member participates.

The most obvious way to participate in a small group is to open your mouth and speak. Small groups are meant to be a conversation, and you cannot have a conversation when people are not talking. So, if you are not participating, you need to realize that you are hurting your group, and therefore hurting yourself.

Perhaps the most frequent reason people are afraid of speaking in a small group is that they are afraid of not having the right answer. They worry that if they do not sound like a theologian, they will be laughed out of the group. It is important to remember that often giving the "right" answer is not necessarily as helpful as giving the "real" answer. Just give the best and most honest answer you can. If you do not know what the "right" answer is, odds are some other people in your group don't either. Your courage to speak up might just spark a group conversation that benefits everyone.

Of course, giving the "real" answer is not always easy. It may reveal to the group that you are less than perfect—imagine their surprise! A healthy sense of vulnerability will benefit the group. How will your group grow when no one is willing to share how he or she needs to grow?

Another way to speak up in your small group is to ask questions. Good questions can ignite great small group conversations. You are not the only one in the group trying to apply God's word to everyday life, and if you have a question, it is very likely that someone else in your group may be wondering the same thing. Remember that the best questions are often the ones about real-life situations, not outlandish hypothetical ones.

Another key to participating in a small group is serving. Peter says:

> As each has received a gift, use it to serve one another, as good stewards of God's varied grace: whoever speaks, as one who speaks oracles of God; whoever serves, as one who serves by the strength that God supplies—in order that in everything God may be glorified

through Jesus Christ. To him belong glory and dominion forever and ever. Amen. (1 Pet. 4:10–11)

These verses remind us that every Christian has received a gift that he or she is responsible for using in the service of others. Give careful thought to how God has gifted you and then seek to use that gift to serve your small group.

Are you gifted in hospitality? Maybe you can host the group in your house, organize the food, or organize an activity for the group. Are you gifted in encouragement? Maybe you can do something each week to encourage another member of the group. Are you gifted in administration? Maybe you can offer to help the leader by creating a group roster and coming up with an easy method for sharing the group's prayer requests. The possibilities are endless. The real question is, are you going to use your gift to benefit the group?

Pursue

Your role in your small group will extend far beyond a weekly meeting because small groups are not events; they are people that God has called you to love. If the goal of small groups is to spur one another on toward love and good deeds, then there are many ways to pursue this goal with your small group more than just once a week.

Some members of the group will be older and more mature in the faith; they should actively pursue helping those in the group who are younger or weaker in the faith. As Titus 2 instructs us, the older men should be training the younger men, and the older women should be discipling the younger women. This is not an activity that can be limited to one night a week. As for those in the group that are younger in the faith, they should actively pursue such instruction and discipleship.

Pursuing others for the common goal of spiritual growth is not limited to relationships where one is older in the faith, and one is younger. Small groups will provide countless opportunities to run the race of faith side-by-side, but many of them will require an intentional pursuit of others.

Two examples of these types of opportunities are encouragement and accountability. As a small group participant, you should be actively looking for openings to encourage others. This encouragement could take a variety of forms, from a care package to a simple text message, but it will always involve a person who has their eyes open and is looking for someone to encourage. Small groups will also provide opportunities for accountability, but again these chances will be wasted unless we are actively pursuing others.

FROM HANDICAPPED TO HEALTHY

If your body only has one working part, you have a serious problem. In fact, many times it only takes one part of your body to malfunction for you to be in dire straits. In order to be healthy, the body of Christ needs every part to fulfill its role.

If you are in a small group, you have a role to play, even if you are not the leader. As we defined it, your job is to "actively use your spiritual gifts to support the small group leader and work for the benefit of the group." Make sure the group is rightly prioritized in your life. Diligently prepare for your group each week. Use your gifts to participate in the life of the group. Actively pursue relationships and mutual encouragement even outside of the small group meetings.

If everyone in your small group commits to doing these things, your group will move from handicapped to healthy. You will experience the joy and productivity of a body where every member is doing its job. But let me close with this warning; if you prove yourself to be faithful and consistent in doing these things, you may be recruited to be a small group leader.

Chapter 3

A CASE FOR SERMON-BASED SMALL GROUPS

Maximizing Your Application of God's Word

John Fabarez

The United States is the largest exporter of food in the world, producing over 300 billion pounds of food every year.[2] It makes sense that an industrial powerhouse like the US should be able to produce more than enough food for all its 335 million residents. Yet, with almost one thousand pounds of food for every mouth, it is sad that nearly 34 million people in the United States suffer some form of food shortage.[3] What makes the situation even worse is that 119 billion pounds of food is thrown away and never eaten. Let me put that massive amount of food in perspective: that translates to 130 billion meals and over 400 billion dollars down the drain. This much food is enough to feed every hungry person in America three meals a day, and then do the same for 85 million people after that!

While it is tragic that almost 40% of all edible food goes to waste in our country, it is even more tragic that many Christians can receive such good biblical teaching regularly, yet never mature in their Christian lives; while many people never enjoy the blessings of Bible teaching at all! For those with a diet consisting of abundant truth, much more than 40% of it may go to waste because it is never correctly digested.

Our appetite for biblical truth can outpace our ability to digest what we are learning. This is a good problem to have, but it is a problem nonetheless. It is hard to blame the average churchgoer who is never exhorted to discuss, meditate, study, and apply what they hear on Sunday to their daily lives. Christians must be trained to hear, digest, and apply God's word.

The apostle James instructed the suffering Jewish Christians to "be doers of the word, and not hearers only, deceiving yourselves" (Jas. 1:22). Many Christians hear solid biblical exposition on a weekly basis, but they never put what they hear into practice. Perhaps this is because they are never encouraged to discuss and apply any of the sermon's contents. And the Lord Jesus himself warned that if anyone hears his words and does not do them, he "will be like a foolish man who built his house on the sand. And the rain fell, and the flood came, and the winds blew and beat against that house, and it fell, and great was the fall of it" (Matt. 7:26–27). It is not enough to comprehend biblical truth. Faithful Christians must live it out in their daily lives. Sadly, we do not become godly Christians through biblical osmosis. In fact, increasing knowledge without a corresponding growth in love and concern for others can be counterproductive (1 Cor. 8:1). We need to do the hard work of meditating on the truth of God's word if we ever hope to be transformed into the image of Christ (2 Cor. 3:18). In the context of the local church, this kind of study is most effective when done in a group setting, where Christians can be sharpened and encouraged by each other.

Think of all the time your pastor spends every week studying, praying, and preparing to preach God's word to your congregation. If he spends twelve hours weekly, he will prepare sermons for 600 hours a year. As he labors, prays, and meditates on what would be best for you to know and do, are you putting in any effort to apply what he preaches? What do you have to show for all that you have been taught? Jesus explained that those who know more will be held responsible for that knowledge (Luke 12:48). Well-taught Christians who remain spiritually immature are in a tragic situation of their own making. Is there a way to avoid this negative evaluation from Christ?

We will make the case that the best method for digesting the preached truth of God's word is in a sermon-based small group. A weekly meeting that is structured around a mature Christian leader who guides the group through a series of questions that come from the most recent sermon, which the whole group heard that weekend from their pastor.

WHAT IS A SERMON-BASED SMALL GROUP?

The church in Jerusalem exploded in size in the first few days and weeks after Pentecost. The book of Acts records that over three thousand souls were saved and baptized on the first day (Acts 2:41). What an amazing spiritual harvest! And what a massive task of leadership and discipleship lay ahead for the twelve appointed apostles.

Right away, these Christians were devoting themselves to the apostles' teaching and fellowship with each other (Acts 2:42). During these self-forgetful glory days of the church, everyone was sharing what they had to cover the needs of others. And they spent significant time together, going to the temple and to each other's homes "day by day" (Acts 2:46). God built his church through the thriving discipleship of these new believers. And it was only natural for them to spend time together beyond the corporate worship in the temple led by the apostles. It was logistically impossible for the apostles to visit all those meetings, let alone lead all those home small groups. Luke records that these fellowship groups formed because of the generous hearts of these followers of Christ who wanted more people to receive forgiveness from sin through repentance: "And the Lord added to their number day by day those who were being saved" (Acts 2:47).

Can the modern church learn anything about small group ministry from this inspired account? Absolutely. A multitude of fellowship groups exist that encourage the sharing of food, prayer, and conversation between believers. Yet the key feature often missing from many small groups is the one Luke mentioned first, "they devoted themselves to the apostles' teaching." (Acts 2:42). The inspired and inerrant word of God is the foundation of a sermon-based small group, and the topic and text are determined by the exposition of Scripture delivered by the pastor in his most recent sermon. Three important things should be in place for an effective sermon-based small group.

First, a sermon-based small group is most effective when all its participants are a part of the same local church under the same pastoral leadership and teaching. In Acts 2, there was only one local church with twelve highly competent leaders, and all the Jerusalem Christians were a part of it. As the gospel moved from Judea and Samaria to the ends of the earth, new local churches were established and built upon the leadership and authority of the apostles (Eph. 2:20). Then, those apostles appointed leaders to oversee the congregations in their absence. The New Testament authors call these leaders elders, overseers, and shepherds (Acts 20:28, Eph. 4:11, 1 Tim. 3:1–2, Titus 1:5, 1 Pet. 5:1–2). Throughout the epistles, the participants in each local church are instructed to submit to their spiritual leaders, be generous with them, show them honor, and make their job a joy (Heb. 13:17; 1 Tim. 5:17; Gal. 6:6). It is practically difficult for sermon-based small groups to be filled with people from different local churches who have different pastors teaching different things. Paul likens the local church to a body, with individual parts gifted by the Holy Spirit for the growth and health of the whole body (1 Cor. 12:12–14). Just as it is natural for body parts to work together, it is natural for participants in local churches to focus on loving others in their church. This looks like spending time together and speaking the truth in love so that all will grow in Christlike maturity (Eph. 4:15–16). Paul rebukes some Corinthian church participants for selfishly retreating from church life because they aren't happy about their gifting (1 Cor. 12:15–16). Sadly, many people in our local churches do not engage in church life because they are dissatisfied with their church body or their own gifts. Many never even enter small groups because of the self-centered introspection that Paul condemns in this passage. Sermon-based small groups can be an excellent solution to this problem.

Second, a sermon-based small group should be guided by qualified leaders who are trained and competent to lead others. Every Christian should sense the duty to grow in Christlikeness and knowledge of the Scriptures. Yet, those leading small groups should feel a more significant pressure to be an approved worker handling the Bible (2 Tim. 2:15). They should aim to be competent to counsel and instruct others (Rom. 15:14). Even the early church servants (sometimes called "deacons") were held to high character qualifications (Acts 6:3; 1 Tim. 3:8–13). Paul told Timothy to put his servants through a period of testing before they took on more responsibilities (1 Tim. 3:10). This is instructive for those appointing small group leaders, they need to make sure their leaders are above reproach, have a good reputation, and a godly character.

Sermon-based small groups allow everyone to share and converse about the insights they learned from the sermon. Having a set time every week to meet with other Christians for encouragement, exhortation, and fellowship is an amazing gift from God! In settings like this, it is practically helpful to have someone who takes the leadership role so that conversations stay on track. However, leaders should intentionally facilitate discussion instead of dominating the conversation. Small groups are not the time to re-preach the sermon. In a healthy group, the leader should develop an influential relationship with the participants, and if multiple mature Christians are in the group they can take turns leading the conversation. Because these sermon-based small groups are a part of the ministry of a local church under the leadership of its pastors, small group leaders and pastors should regularly communicate with each other about the unique needs, challenges, and growth of each small group.

Third, a sermon-based small group should direct all its participants to put the sermon into practice in their daily lives. "Where application begins, there the sermon begins," is the oft-quoted ministry insight from the Prince of Preachers, Charles Spurgeon.[4] Sermon-based small groups provide participants the time and space to digest the sermon. Small group leaders and participants should contemplate questions like: What did the sermon push me to do? How did the sermon change my thinking? What sins did this sermon encourage me to put to death? Who are the people that the sermon urged me to love? And how does God want me to change because of this sermon? Pastors are contemplating these kinds of questions during their sermon preparation time, and it is a good practice for Christians to do the same after they hear the sermon. Good questions can drive home the application intended by the text studied at church. It is ideal for whoever preached the sermon in church to write questions for all the small groups to discuss. But if a pastor has not provided questions, the leader should be responsible for writing out discussion questions with appropriate Scriptures before the group meets.

THE BENEFITS OF BELONGING TO A SERMON-BASED SMALL GROUP

Counting God's blessings and benefits for obedience to his word can be an encouraging and life-giving exercise (Ps. 103:2–5). This list is not comprehensive, but it is a helpful reminder of what God is doing for you and others through participation in a sermon-based small group.

First, a sermon-based small group provides the intimate Christian community we crave. Anti-social behavior has become the cultural norm in the 21st century thanks to technological advances and decreases in community life. In 2000, Robert Putnam wrote the book Bowling Alone, which exposed the hyper-individualized nature of American culture.[5] Over the last two decades, the anti-social trends have only worsened with the rise and triumph of smartphones and social media. The church is one of the only institutions that will continue to promote and value face-to-face relationships, no matter the cost. The COVID-19 pandemic in 2020 proved that retreat from community life has devastating consequences. Local churches will naturally satisfy one of the deepest felt needs for community. However, the Christian community is much more than a social club that helps its members find a sense of satisfaction or identity. It is the organic body of believers in Christ who are linked together by a common faith and allegiance to God, the Lord Jesus Christ, and his Scriptures (Eph. 1:22–23; 4:4–6; 4:15–16). Jesus prayed to the Father for his disciples to enjoy this kind of unity, asking "that they may be one, even as we are one" (John 17:11). Over time, small groups of Christians should develop the kind of affection that can only be compared to a family. Paul expressed this kind of family love for those he ministered to, calling them his "joy" and his "crown of boasting before the Lord" and his "glory" (1 Thess. 2:19). His deep love for the Ephesian Christians was on display when he wept with them on the docks at Miletus while saying a final farewell (Acts 20:19, 31, 37–38). Most Christians long for this kind of deep connection with others in their church, and this kind of love is possible for groups that have faithfully loved one another over time.

Second, a sermon-based small group provides long-term accountability for its participants to grow in godliness. Ultimately, one of the most important things you can do for the Christians in your life is to encourage them to be godly. You need other Christians, and they need you, as illustrated by the body metaphor in 1 Corinthians 12. God sovereignly placed you where you are (Acts 17:26) and within the church family you have, so that you would love the people in front of you. We need others who will sharpen us (Prov. 27:17). If as Christians we are living in ongoing sin, it is hard to hide if we are blessed with a small group that has intimate knowledge of our situation and regularly checks in with us. How many sins would be avoided if every participant had accountability relationships where they honestly confessed their sins to one another and prayed for each other (Jas. 5:16)? Your sermon-based small group will bring about knowledge and confession of sin, which can set up one-on-one conversations about repentance from sin (Gal. 6:1–2). This is God's good design for his people, and a sermon-based small group can help accomplish this kind of accountability. When a small group stays together for an extended period, they will experience many spiritual tragedies, but even more spiritual victories together!

Third, a sermon-based small group contributes to the unity of your local church. When a group functions correctly, it will fight against the threat of disunity with every meeting. As every sermon-based small group in the church works through the same material and biblical texts, the church should be growing in the same areas. If the sermon is about anger and reconciliation, the whole church is discussing how to restore broken relationships with one another. If a sermon is about pride and humility, each small group will do introspective work to ensure their motives are pure. If the sermon was about prayer, all the people should be moved to start praying with more zeal in the following weeks. In other words, when the church hears sermons and then discusses the application with one another, the whole church will be moved to action together. The early church displayed this kind of supernatural unity when they met daily, breaking bread together and sharing their resources so that every Christian was cared for. King David proclaimed, "Behold, how good and pleasant it is when brothers dwell in unity" (Ps. 133:1). Relationally united small groups are a regular source of blessing for all parties involved.

Fourth, a sermon-based small group encourages its participants to follow the leadership of its local church pastors. Every Sunday morning, pastors stand up and deliver messages from the Scriptures to their local churches. You cannot separate teaching from leadership, as Paul illustrates in 1 Timothy 3:2. When expository preaching is doctrinally deep and pastorally applicational, congregations are directed by their shepherds to follow the Chief Shepherd. Hopefully, you desire more people in your church to follow your pastor's teaching, leadership, and example (Heb. 13:7). One excellent way to do this is through the ministry of sermon-based small groups, where everyone is discussing how they can do what they were told on Sunday morning. Just as every infantry unit in the army thrives under the direction and commonality of shared goals, local churches are like units in the army of God doing the will of their Commander-in-Chief. When churches are faithful to this form of fellowship, it is easier to mobilize the congregation to accomplish God's tasks for them.

Fifth, a sermon-based small group does not suffer the ebbs and flows of a small group searching for content in books, societal issues, and current events. Certain small group models utilize Christian books or Sunday

School curriculum to guide conversations. Depending on the quality of the training materials, this can have some value and is appropriate for some small groups. But using the weekend sermon for guidance in the conversations has a natural advantage because it is a consistent form that does not change as the season of ministry unfolds. Yet, groups enjoy the variety of topics and texts the preacher chooses. It is helpful for groups to continue to meet when a guest preacher delivers a special sermon disconnected from the pastor's sermon series so they can talk about unique topics.

Sixth, a sermon-based small group should produce a mature company of believers that can break off and lead their own groups. God uses the regular ministry of the Bible to sanctify his saints. Paul prayed and strove to present everyone mature in Christ through his preaching (Col. 1:28). Your pastor certainly asks God for this to be true in your church regularly. If you don't believe me, just ask him! When Jesus urged his disciples to make more disciples, he left a model and mission for the whole church to multiply. It is only natural for groups that grow in depth of knowledge and love for one another to attract others to their group. Once a small group is no longer small, leaders should identify other potential leaders to take over a portion of the group (see Chapter 11). If you have spent years investing in disciples of Christ, you should expect them to mature into the kind of people who can lead others. One of the marks of success for any sermon-based small group is that it is growing and multiplying.

YOUR RESPONSIBILITIES IN A SERMON-BASED SMALL GROUP

Along with the great blessings of being in a small group, God also wants all participants to take responsibility for a few things that impact the spiritual growth of the whole group. As you approach being a part of a sermon-based small group as a leader or participant, these five responsibilities should help you make the most of the time you invest in your group.

First, commit to being a part of a sermon-based small group for an extended period of time. This kind of commitment goes against the grain of the highly mobile, consumeristic society we minister in. We should make decisions about church and Christian fellowship with other people in mind (Phil. 2:3-4). Ultimately, long-term commitments to particular local churches and small groups will promote abundant fruitfulness. Also, building the habit of attending and connecting with others through small groups is very valuable for those raising children. It communicates to those young hearts that their parents are serious about God and his church, which will one day lay the foundation for their commitment to the body of Christ. Some small groups meet simultaneously as children's groups during the school year, while others meet year-round. Whatever your church structure necessitates, choose to be a part of a group for an extended season, and don't look for an exit. Even when there are relational problems and conflict, pursue reconciliation in the Lord (Matt. 5:23–24; Phil. 4:2–3) and keep loving one another as you commit to spiritual growth together. If God blesses your group with more people, you may be forced into a change because your group multiplies. Praise God for the new opportunity and people he has brought into your life to love.

Second, come to your small group prepared to discuss the sermon. You are not ready to engage in a sermon-based small group if you have not listened to the sermon! There will be some rare occasions when you can attend the small group time but cannot listen to the preaching event on the weekend. Use your church's media to watch the sermon before coming to small groups. But most weeks, you will discuss a sermon you just heard days or hours beforehand. As a small group "participant," not a "spectator," you have the responsibility to talk about the sermon, so you should take good notes during the preaching event and bring those to the small group time. Further, you can review any application questions that the pastor wrote, before you discuss them in the larger group. For husbands and wives, talking through some of the questions together in the car after the sermon or before the small group time can be very fruitful.

Third, stay on task by following the questions instead of making the small group about an unrelated topic. Small group participants and leaders should do their best to stay on topic. If your small group regularly gets off track, it is not following the leadership of your pastor through his sermon and application questions. Your group time may devolve into a political conversation or turn to discussing current events. While this is not all bad, it is out of place and not meeting the goals of a sermon-based small group. Try your best to consecrate the hour a week you spend discussing your pastor's sermon to focus on digesting that message with its application in your daily life. Your group will grow in Christlikeness and holiness if you are faithful to stay on topic, week in and week out. All those other conversations are good to have another time. If members want to stay late to talk after small group time is over, that is a sign of a healthy group. The more casual conversations your group can have about daily life, the better. But during group time make sure you do everything you can to digest God's message for your church through focused discussion and prayer about the weekend sermon.

Fourth, care for the people in your group like you would for your family. If you commit to a small group for an extended period of time, you will visit your fellow members in the hospital, pray for their prodigal children, and celebrate a member's baptism. At some point, you may even stand on a stage to eulogize them at their funeral. As a group, you will share those significant life events because you started by sharing life's minor and routine events. You sat together at church, watched their son's football games, and attended their daughter's piano recitals. This is the kind of church-family life that we all crave! You should aim to be that kind of church-family for those in your small group. Don't be guilty of closing your heart to your brothers and sisters with needs (1 John 3:17), but instead abound in generosity to those people in your group when they are struggling, sick, or grieving. Planning activities or meals outside your regular small group time will help your relationships grow deeper in a different setting.

Fifth, pray for the spiritual growth of the individuals God has sovereignly placed in your group. All the conversations, prayers, and shared activities with your group members should point to the goal of becoming more like Christ. Start by praying for each other and with each other. Most small groups benefit from a short time to share prayer requests and praise reports before or after the small group discussion time. Utilize the technology at your disposal to encourage faithful prayer throughout the week. Most of all, follow the example of this godly first-century saint:

> Epaphras, who is one of you, a servant of Christ Jesus, greets you, always struggling on your behalf in his prayers, that you may stand mature and fully assured in all the will of God. (Col. 4:12)

Aim for something greater than friendships through your sermon-based small group. Ask God for more sanctification, personal devotion, humility, selflessness, and sacrificial love in your group. By so doing, we will all fulfill God's command for our good:

> And let us consider how to stir up one another to love and good works, not neglecting to meet together, as is the habit of some, but encouraging one another, and all the more as you see the Day drawing near. (Heb. 10:24–25)

Chapter 4

COMMON PITFALLS

How to Solve Small Group Problems

Mark Kelley

People have problems. And when you have people in a room with other people, you have compounding problems! Therefore, it is no surprise that many pitfalls threaten to contaminate the health and derail the positive impact of small groups. Most small group members have experienced these dangers before. The good news is that there are biblical solutions, and they are surprisingly straightforward. This chapter sets out to not only identify specific solutions to the most common problems but to also provide practical steps to troubleshoot any given pitfall.[6]

To begin, I'd like to propose a simple key: *people in small groups must be in agreement on the purpose of small groups.* Members must agree to a common set of terms and values regarding what a small group is and how it should operate. A "pitfall" would then be anything that takes a person or group off the course that leads toward achieving their shared purpose.

The purpose of small groups is for *Christians to connect with one another in order to grow relationships with God and others through discussion of Scripture, accountability, and fellowship.* If small group leaders and participants can get on board with this set of objectives and stick to them, then many pitfalls can be avoided altogether. And, when a pitfall does occur, the solution can be found in getting back on track with the purpose statement.

The problems that plague small groups are numerous. In order to work through such a broad topic, I have identified some of the most common pitfalls and placed them into three categories: (1) Personal Problems, (2) Group Problems, (3) Leadership Problems.

God does amazing things through the small group dynamic as the Bible reminds us: "Above all, keep loving one another earnestly, since love covers a multitude of sins. Show hospitality to one another without grumbling. As each has received a gift, use it to serve one another, as stewards of God's varied grace" (1 Pet. 4:8–10). Let's make sure that the following common pitfalls do not get in the way of us accomplishing these important goals.

PERSONAL PROBLEMS

Personal problems concern an individual and often his or her sin, which becomes exposed in the small group setting. Consequently, most solutions to the problems in this category will inevitably involve a face-to-face appointment between meetings, where the goal is to come alongside the group member and help them to see his or her fault (Gal. 6:1–2). The recommended solutions will provide not only a set of temporary remedies to help navigate the immediate challenge in a given situation, but they will ultimately help the leader hone in on the lasting changes that need to take place on a deeper, personal level.

Self-Promotion

This pitfall involves people who use the platform of the small group setting to inflate their reputation. They speak in such a way as to put themselves on display for all to see and admire. They may even tickle the ears of their audience with ultra "godly" zeal, leaving the group to applaud their artificial spirituality (3 John 9). While the content of what they say may at times be true, the motive behind this kind of self-promotion is typically a sinful desire to exaggerate their own reputation.

It is important that the leader carefully detect this problem and take the necessary action to solve it. To provide a temporary solution, avoid praising the self-promoting person, and in turn, jump to another person to share an answer. The self-promoter is looking for admiration, and rather than condoning the group's applause for him, the leader must shift the attention back to the topic and give the floor to someone else in the group. However, what ultimately needs to happen is a between-meetings conversation in which the effect of the person's comments is addressed. Self-promoters need someone to humbly and lovingly help them see that what they are doing is wrong and that there may be pride below the surface that needs to be addressed. This should be dealt with quickly, considering how unloving it would be to allow this behavior to continue without addressing the core problem in a timely manner.

"Correct" but Insincere Answers

People who have been around church for any length of time quickly learn what are often referred to as "Sunday school answers." These responses successfully answer the question without ever plunging beneath the surface. This allows individuals to be superficial and closed off to the group. If you never reach out to people who provide these types of answers, then they may faithfully attend the small group without ever engaging in the profitable work of sharing from the heart and even, when appropriate, confessing sin.

It is imperative, therefore, that small group leaders ask probing and open-ended questions during the group meeting. The art of asking good questions is one that every small group leader should work to master. This involves following up a superficial answer with further questions like: "That's a good answer, but could you tell us why that is the case for you personally?" or "Can you give us an example of that from your own life?" However, these questions only provide a temporary solution to a deeper issue. Begin the process of solving this pattern by purposing to get to know that person better. This may be all it takes to get the superficial participant to open up in the group setting. Often though, the problem involves some form of hypocrisy—putting on a righteous front on the outside and leaving the ugly, sinful reality hidden behind a facade.

"Sharing" with an Agenda

Sometimes a small group member shows up with an agenda different than that of the corporate goal. These people may arrive at small groups eager to bring up the most recent political drama, tasty bits of controversial news, or, why a favorite NFL team never fails to disappoint. Whatever the group's intended topic of discussion, they are ready to find a way to voice their personal bit. The content of their discussion may not be sinful, but it is clear that they are taking the group off course to their own desired topic.

This problem can be solved temporarily by bringing the point of discussion back to the original topic—even if a diplomatic and gentle interruption needs to take place. But again, this is an instance where having a conversation outside of the group is needed to help the person see the reality of what he or she is doing. Ultimately, the goal is to help them shift their agenda so that they will come to the small group with the intent to reach the mutual goal of "connecting with one another…"

Subtly Tearing Down Others

People can do terrible damage with their words as the Bible reminds us:

> And the tongue is a fire, a world of unrighteousness. The tongue is set among our members, staining the whole body, setting on fire the entire course of life, and set on fire by hell. For every kind of beast and bird, of reptile and sea creature, can be tamed and has been tamed by mankind, but no human being can tame the tongue. It is a restless evil, full of deadly poison. With it we bless our Lord and Father, and with it we curse people who are made in the likeness of God. From the same mouth come blessing and cursing. My brothers, these things ought not to be so. (Jas. 3:6–10)

Unfortunately, a small group can become the setting where group members use their tongues to subtly hurt others. It is easy to talk about the problems of other people in response to discussion questions, but the intended goal of small groups is for application and personal interaction with the text. Work hard to ensure your group does not become a context for tearing down instead of building up.

When damaging words are spoken, the leader should redirect the question back to the person who is pointing out the faults of others. Ask them about how they have stumbled in the same area. This problem, like the others, is likely to continue unless a time is set to discuss the problem with the person and help him or her see the damage that can be caused by such comments. Help that person not only identify the sin of their words but also work with them on how to use their words to build up others. Small group members should be reminded to approach the small group setting with the premeditated goal of actually bringing encouraging and positive words about at least one other person. They should bring an agenda of trying to use their words to "give grace" to one another (Eph. 4:29).

Summary

Sin is the common thread in this category. Heart issues are behind each one of these "personal" pitfalls. Therefore, as a general rule, the overarching solution for issues in this category is *repentance*. When a personal problem in a small group setting is encountered, the solution can in most cases be traced back to a particular sin, which needs to be dealt with, seen for what it is, and turned from. Though other pitfalls could be discussed within this category, the overarching solution for them all is this: personal problems require repentance.[7]

GROUP PROBLEMS

Some problems center around the social dynamic of a small group.

Many of these problems originate with individuals, but what sets them apart from the previous category is that they take form in group settings. These pitfalls can negatively affect the small group in a major way, so implementing wisdom here is crucial.

Conversation Dominators

You know him or her well. This is the person who simply loves answering every possible question with long-winded answers. The conversation dominator may be an eloquent speaker and may even have a good grasp of biblical information. Unsurprisingly, they dominate the conversation because they always have more to say than everyone else and they sound good saying it. A small group leader needs to take action when this kind of participant arrives on the scene, or else the intended purpose of "connecting with one another in order to deepen relationships with God and others…" will be lost.

To deal with conversation dominators, approach them before or after the meeting and lay out the purpose for small groups. Show them how they can play a major role in helping the group realize its purpose, rather than taking it off course. If they can catch the vision of why there is a room full of people with open Bibles (realizing that they have assembled not just to hear from him or her), they can do great good for the group. Instead of using their gifts to simply talk a lot about what they know, they can harness their gifts to partner with the leader in facilitating conversation. This sort of person can even be commissioned with special tasks during the meetings or in the absence of the leader (more on this later).

Wallflowers

People who talk too little (or not at all) present us with a problem as concerning as the people who talk too much! Opposite of the conversation dominator, the wallflower will sit back and not say a word. They may not speak up for a number of reasons: perhaps they are shy, they are intimidated (especially by the conversation dominator), they do not want to misinterpret a Bible verse, or maybe they just do not want to sound dumb. Regardless, because the wallflower is not talking, the small group is failing to achieve its purpose of *connecting* with one another because this person is excluded from the conversation.

As the leader, once you become aware of the wallflowers, you can work to get them involved. After a relationship has been established, a simple and effective way to help this person is to contact them before the gathering and ask them to pull out their discussion sheet and tell you the answer they have written down for one of the questions. Then affirm the answer and encourage them by expressing that their answer would be of help to the rest of the group. Let them know you will likely call on them when you get to that question during the meeting. In many cases, the wallflower will rise to the occasion! Of course, when they do speak up during small group time, you should be quick to encourage them. In certain cases, it may be appropriate to call on specific people who have not been talking during the small group session (whether you called them ahead of time or not). With the possible exception of someone who is brand new to the group, the goal is to get everyone interacting with one another.

Overly Emotional or Disruptive

If you lead a small group for any length of time, participants in your group will inevitably experience minor disappointments and even major trials: the loss of a job, eviction from a home, the death of a family member, or any number of difficulties. There are legitimate and expected unhappy emotions tied to situations like these, and there is a good chance small group members will enter the group session with the weight of one of these trials clearly wearing them down. They may even walk through the door with tears streaming down their face!

The small group is certainly there to help in this time of need, but these situations must be handled wisely or the whole time allotted to discussing the application questions could end up being spent talking about one individual's problem.[8] Right off the bat, you should gather the group together and lead a time of prayer for the hurting individual. The comfort and encouragement provided during this time may be all the emotional help the person needs. However, there is a good chance that further support is required—and the small group is there to provide this level of help as well. After corporate prayer, it may be appropriate for the leader (or a qualified member) to pull this individual out of the room and use the rest of the time to minister to them one-on-one. The leader should listen to them, talk with them, pray with them, and even cry with them, for as long as it takes. This is an opportune time to signal a co-leader or responsible attendee to step up and take the reins of the discussion in the leader's absence.

Gossip

It certainly comes as no surprise that people are prone to gossip!

The Proverbs remind us, "The words of a whisperer are like delicious morsels" (Prov. 18:8). Unfortunately, people sometimes capitalize on the social dynamic of the small group to share dramatic morsels of information about others behind their backs. The temptation to disguise gossip about others in the form of prayer requests and concern for others exists. However, the corporate setting of the small group is not the appropriate place to discuss the sins, mistakes, or crises of others.

Therefore, when you detect gossip, act quickly by shutting it down. Ideally, the intuitive and proactive leader will identify questions that lend themselves toward gossip and warn the group before they are even asked to answer. This may stop gossip before it even starts. Group members should all be aware of the *purpose* for small groups—which does not involve the airing out of the sin of others, but rather, at the appropriate times calls for the individual confession of personal sins, which in turn should fuel the personal resolve and mutual accountability to love God and others more.

Debate

Debate is not always bad; in fact, it can be good and healthy! A little tension or argument is not inherently evil, but a well-intentioned debate can quickly become quarrelsome and aggressive, taking the group off course, and destroying relationships in the process. Debates can also be incredibly interesting for two or three people, while being tedious and unhelpful for everyone else. When the conversation takes this sort of a turn, the slippery slide into a dangerous pitfall begins.

The small group leader must be wise in the way they handle

the situation. Leaders are the moderators of the group and should intervene when it is time to provide clarity, answers, or simply move the conversation along. A quick and appeasing solution is to tell the group that you are going to shift the conversation back to the application questions but will stick around after the meeting to continue the discussion on the debated topic. Then, those who are interested in continuing to dialog on the issue can stay, and those who are not interested are not forced to be a part of it. Either way, take great care to handle the situation with grace and wisdom. It would be a tragedy to win the debate but lose the relationship with one of your small group members. Furthermore, it is helpful and wise to follow up (or transition) a debate past mere information and on to biblical application and personal transformation. Ultimately, you want to help people see the need to not simply talk about the Bible, but to talk about the Bible *so that* a love for God and others can be cultivated and enhanced.

Heresy

Heresy is a belief that does not align with biblical truth. Don't be alarmed when heresy is spoken; it is going to happen in your small group whether by accident, ignorance, or misunderstanding. Remember that not all "heretical statements" are created equal. The small group leader needs to have a discerning ear to identify and field the various kinds of heretical statements as they are expressed within the group. Some "inaccurate" statements are inconsequential and insignificant. In those cases, avoid the temptation to see yourself as the theological policeman whose job it is to nitpick every word spoken. On the other hand, some statements are serious contradictions of biblical truth. When these statements are made, you must take responsibility to ensure that the conversations stay within the doctrinal boundaries of the church you are representing.

Heresy can be common in the small group setting because the social element provides every person in the group with the platform to speak—whether or not they have studied the passage or even listened to the sermon being discussed. This can become a major problem because false assumptions, textual misunderstanding, faulty application, and a variety of other inaccuracies can creep into the middle of a discussion that is intended to provide truth, right understanding, and practical application for Christians.

Therefore, small group leaders need to have a plan to address heresy in a diplomatic and wise manner. Since the Bible is the authoritative word of God, this is the first place to turn. Utilize the Bible to correct, clarify, and address serious heretical comments (2 Tim. 3:16–17). A second line of defense can involve a fellow group member who has been prepped ahead of time for such encounters—one who you know to be particularly grounded theologically. He or she can speak up in defense and support of the Scripture being considered and the clarification the leader has proposed. Small groups should be the place where people come and have their wrong thinking corrected and their theological questions answered, not a place where heresy is overlooked, and certainly not a place where heresy is bred!

Summary

Unlike "personal problems," sin is not necessarily the driving factor behind "group problems." Many of these problems naturally arise due to the context of a group setting. These issues just need wise and purposeful intervention. The commonality permeating this whole category of pitfalls is a lack of execution of the purpose of small groups. As a general rule, the overarching solution for any pitfall in the "group problem" category is aligning with the vision for small groups. If the conversation dominator, the wallflower, the debater, or any other person in this category, can get on board with the terms and vision—understanding why we engage in small groups and how he or she can personally aid (or hinder) that goal—then the majority of these problems will be solved! As with the previous category, this is not the case a hundred percent of the time, but it is true for most instances.

LEADERSHIP PROBLEMS

Every small group needs a leader. Leading a group is exciting and rewarding, but it comes with its own set of challenges. And when the small group leader fails to lead well, they can negatively impact the whole group. Not surprisingly then, there are numerous pitfalls we could classify as "leadership problems." And we should be prayerful and careful to avoid them. Half the battle with the pitfalls in this category is identifying the problem; the solutions are simple.

Small group leadership is the work of actively guiding the group in a positive and constructive direction, not simply steering it away from snags. This is an art. If leading a small group were merely a science, leaders could just follow a set formula and achieve the desired result every time. That is obviously not the case. Leading a small group requires a certain finesse. Thoughtfully consider the following scenarios and evaluate yourself honestly regarding each situation.

Allowing Rabbit Trails

It is amazing how fast a conversation can take a turn into no man's land, leaving you scratching your head and asking, "How did we get here?" Rabbit trails have plagued small groups for ages; however, not all rabbit trails are to be avoided. In fact, you may want to strategically encourage certain variant conversations to continue for a period of time. You may find that the unexpected topic is helpful and actually engages those who were previously checked out of the conversation. It might be something as significant as a clarification of what it means to rightly respond to the gospel or how to know we are truly children of God. Some of these unplanned conversations can have an eternally important impact.

By contrast, some rabbit trails are not good at all. Leaders should be responsible for where the small group discussion goes. If it goes in a direction that it should not, or into a collateral topic for too long, it is the leader's job to rein it in. You must not let other people steer the discussion wherever they choose for it to go. Leaders have the plan and must direct the conversation according to that plan. Leaders can take a number of paths to arrive at their goal, but it is their job to ensure the group eventually gets there. These are times when the leader must utilize wisdom and discernment in aiming to achieve the ultimate small group goals, even through off-topic conversations.

Abandoning the Discussion Questions

You can imagine how frustrating it would be for your pastor if his carefully constructed discussion questions, intended to drive home the point and application of the sermon, were regularly disregarded or ignored by small group leaders. The questions are thoughtfully designed to evoke a proper application of the truth of the text that was preached. And typically, the questions materialize *after* he has spent significant time studying and preparing his exposition. So, whether by accident or intent, leaders escort their groups into a gaping pitfall when they summarily abandon the prepared questions.

The simple solution is to resolve to work through the questions during the group meeting! And, when the small group strays from the questions, the leader should be there to bring the discussion back on track. Consider how little time it takes for a small group leader to decide to skip the questions, compared to the time it took the pastor to provide the right questions for his congregants to discuss. This of course does not mean that a small group leader's prayerful leadership will not at times rightly conclude that a question should be restated, or that the questions should be reorganized, or clarified.

Spiritually Unprepared Leaders

One element that makes the job of a small group leader particularly challenging is the element of *spiritual leadership*. This entails much more than preparing an outline, communicating with the group, and making sure a home is ready to accommodate guests. Being a spiritual leader requires discipline to live a consistent and godly life. Those who lead small groups are put in a position of authority and endorsed by the pastoral leadership to minister to the people in their care. When a small group leader fails to maintain his or her walk with the Lord, yet continues in a position of spiritual leadership, problems result.

More than anyone else in the group, the leader needs to be

disciplined in his or her relationship with God. This is going to require that leaders seek to live a faithful and godly life. Godliness is not achieved by putting in a few minutes of preparation before small group time. Small group leaders must make sure that they have given themselves time to internalize and practically apply the sermon before showing up to lead a small group.

Uncaring Leaders

Small group leaders are stewards of a group of people, which they are called to love, minister to, and support. Beyond leading the weekly discussion, a small group leader's job is to love the individuals that God has entrusted to their care. This is a sobering responsibility and one that must not be taken lightly. People struggle to really open up with one another when they suspect the person asking the questions is insincere, uncaring, or unloving. Groups can feel distant and unengaged if there is no love present, especially when no love appears to be coming from the leader. Failing to truly care about the people in your group will drag everyone down into a costly pitfall.

To ensure this does not happen, you must actively pursue relationships with the people in your group. When there are sincere relationships, effective *connecting* can happen. However, relationships with people are not instantly formed and they are not always easy to sustain. In fact, loving your people in this way requires a lot of work. And that includes the work of prayer. Sometimes the best way to increase your love for someone (even those who may be difficult to love) is to consistently pray for him or her. It is surprising to see how God will markedly increase your love and genuine concern for the people you pray for regularly.

Not Opening the Bible

The Bible should be opened, read, and consulted in every single small group meeting! It would be a tragedy to not consult God's authoritative and enlightening word during a small group session. As we promote in this book, *sermon-based small groups* will require small group participants to look at the text upon which the sermon was based, as well as a variety of other verses to support the preached text. It is the discussion of Scripture and its application that is the primary means by which people increase in their love for God and others.

Small group leaders need to make sure that the Bible is opened, read, and considered in every small group meeting. Preparing for the meeting will always necessitate locating and becoming familiar with the verses you plan to consult and direct people to during your small group discussion. Accept the responsibility of knowing where you will be going in the Bible—and if it will be limited to the verses listed in the questions, or if you plan to consult additional passages to help guide the discussion.

Avoiding the Spiritual Solutions

The presence of spiritual solutions distinguishes church-based small groups from all other social clubs or support groups. While small groups should strive to meet physical and practical needs, they are designed to do more than that! It would be fantastic for a group to help one of its participants move to a new house or find a job; however, the small group should do more by attending to the spiritual needs of the participants amid life's practical needs. It would be a biblical failure to help someone fix their car, their home, or some other problem, but to leave their soul in need of repair.

Questions like, "How are you *really* doing with this?" "How can we specifically pray for you during this time?" and, "What has God been teaching you in this season of life?" may help take the discussion past the surface level and really address someone's heart. This must be every small group leader's ultimate target. More than meeting an individual's physical needs, leaders need to be concerned and focused on people's spiritual needs.

Leaders Talking Too Much

The small group leader is not there to re-preach the sermon, or to provide a lengthy analysis of the topic at hand. Leaders are there because every group needs a leader—someone who is committed to facilitating the cThe small group leader is not there to re-preach the sermon, or to provide a lengthy analysis of the topic at hand. Leaders are there because every group needs a leader—someone who is committed to facilitating the conversation and providing clarity and direction for the discussion. Leaders need to talk just enough to get the rest of the group interacting and focused on the topic at hand.

It is essential that leaders embrace their role as discussion facilitators. Often, leaders are the ones who tend to have good answers to the questions and may be tempted to share them all. Leaders must be mindful of the pitfall of talking too much and avoid answering every question and talking more than is necessary. Leaders can even implement strategies to keep themselves in check. It may be helpful to include "notes-to-self" as reminders to talk less or to think about who has not shared yet.

Leaders must develop the art of asking open-ended questions. Open-ended questions are posed in such a way that a yes or no answer is not possible. For example, switch "Have you read your Bible this week?" to "What is your current Bible reading routine?" The carefully worded and thought-provoking questions provided by the pastor typically contain questions like this. Your supplemental questions should follow the pattern of being open-ended. This helps foster an atmosphere of discussion, where small group members meaningfully engage with one another's comments rather than merely trying to state the "correct" answers to questions.

Summary

As with the "personal problems" and "group problems," there is an over-arching solution that works for "leadership problems." Generally, every problem within this category stems from a lack of discipline. Whether it is allowing rabbit trails, abandoning the questions, or not being spiritually ready, the solution is most likely found in *being personally and spiritually disciplined.* Being a leader is a challenging task and one that is not effective without discipline. However, when leaders accept discipline as a fundamental responsibility of what they signed up for, they will be able to eagerly embrace the challenge of being used by God as an effective small group leader.

CONCLUSION

We have looked at numerous small group problems and corresponding solutions. Yet, the list of pitfalls contained in this chapter is not exhaustive. When we encounter pitfalls not addressed in this chapter, it will be helpful to utilize our three categories (personal, group, and leadership problems) to diagnose the problem at hand. We can then recall the generalized solutions: repentance, vision casting, and personal discipline.

These three over-arching solutions can bring us back to the key principle established at the beginning of the chapter: know the purpose of small groups and stick to it. Whenever there is a lack of repentance, a lack of alignment with the terms and vision, or a lack of personal discipline, then achieving the common aim will be seriously hindered. But, when we remain on track with the purpose of small groups, we can overcome countless pitfalls and successfully move toward the intended goal.

Chapter 5

BUILDING TRUST

Keys to Authentic Relationships

PJ Berner

We've all been there. You walk into a new small group, and there are awkward introductions, plastered smiles, and nervous handshakes. Small talk ensues for fifteen or twenty minutes, while everyone is gathered around someone's kitchen island with store-bought cookies and a pitcher of coffee. You make the rounds telling the same story about your family and hearing some variation of a similar story from the other couples that you meet.

Then it happens. The leader calls the group together in the living room, and people take the same seats they've occupied each week for years. You anxiously take an open seat and already feel your defenses beginning to rise. This is when they expect you to talk, to open up to a room full of strangers. This is when they expect you to have something profound to say about the discussion questions you didn't know about until five minutes before you walked in the door. This is when they expect you to offer a prayer request to a room full of people you just met an hour ago.

Trust, like your grandma's antique vase, takes a long time to create and only seconds to shatter. Like muscle, it takes time to amass, build, and accumulate. And yet, sometimes, we walk into a small group and sense the expectation that we should be able to bench press 250lbs on the trust bench that first night. So, how do we cultivate a culture of trust within our groups as leaders?

Maybe you're just starting with a brand-new group you've been tasked to lead. Maybe you've been leading a group stuck in the relational shallow end for the last year. Maybe you're leading a group that has established a deep level of confidence and comfort with each other, but now your dynamic has been thrown off by adding two new couples. How do we build the level of trust within our groups that we hope to have? That's what will be addressed in the following pages.

TRUST: WHAT IS IT?

You know what trust looks like and feels like inside a relationship, but could you define what it means to trust another person this way? That's what we're going to attempt to do in this section. Psychologist C.W. Ellison described trust as "an act of dependency upon another person for the fulfillment of biological, psychological, social, or spiritual needs that cannot be met independently. It is subjective confidence in the intentions and ability of another to promote and/or guard one's well-being that leads a person to risk possible harm or loss."[9] At the risk of oversimplifying things, we might put it this way: trust is the expression of dependence upon another person. We find this concept modeled in biblical relationships.

David and Jonathan

These two souls were knit together in a mutual trust that led the future king of Israel to place his security and well-being in the hands of the man everyone assumed would be next to take the throne. In the story of Jonathan and David, we see two friends who depend upon one another for their own needs and, in the case of Jonathan, for the needs of his family and children.

Joab and Abishai

This is a less well-known relationship than that of Jonathan and David, but it provides another excellent example of trust. In 2 Samuel 10, Joab led Israel to battle against the Ammonites and the Syrians. When he realized he was surrounded, he turned to his brother Abishai and devised a plan that would only work if they could genuinely trust one another. He split the army and told Abishai to take some of the men to defend against the Ammonites, and he would take the rest to protect against the Syrians. In 2 Samuel 10:11, he said to his brother, "If the Syrians are too strong for me, then you shall help me, but if the Ammonites are too strong for you, then I will come and help you." This is relational trust in the most intense circumstances.

The Early Church

For a New Testament example, we need not look any further than the earliest days of the church. In Acts 4:32–37, we read of the selflessness and the sacrificial trust of the fledgling body of Christ as everyone was intent on meeting the needs that presented themselves in the flock. The people with means would sell their possessions and bring the money to the Apostles, trusting that they would steward it for the good of the body.

So, what is trust? It's a sacrificial dependence on one or more people while calculating the risk involved and expressing a mutual commitment to the well-being of the others in the relationship. This is what we're after in the context of our small groups, and in the next section, we'll look at why this is so important.

TRUST: WHY DOES IT MATTER?

If your neighborhood is like mine, there are Facebook groups, home security groups, and neighborhood bulletin boards where people post relevant information about the community. One of the more valuable elements of groups like these is the ability to ask for recommendations. Maybe you need a plumber or an electrician, or a good restaurant recommendation for an anniversary dinner. We turn to these community boards and groups because there is something about them we *trust*. Our shared interests cause us to believe that these neighbors have our best interests in mind and vice-versa. I only bring this up to point out that trust is not exclusively Christian.

That said, trust takes on a different level of importance within the church walls, and more specifically in the small group you lead. Authenticity is a prevalent word in our culture today, and that's not a bad thing. We need to be men and women of integrity. We should be the same people behind closed doors as we are at church on Sunday morning. I assume I'm on solid footing to believe that each of you reading this book desires to have authenticity in your small groups. You don't want people to provide the Sunday school answer if they aren't sure why it's the correct answer. However, authenticity is dependent on trust.

Consider what we're asking of the people participating in our small groups. We're asking them to sit down with fourteen or fifteen other people and answer questions about how the previous weekend's sermon is lived out in their lives. We're asking them to share their struggles and convictions. We're asking them to confess sin and to be open to correction and accountability. We're asking them to share prayer requests. On an authenticity scale, we're asking for 10/10. Without building trust, we'll never get any of these things. If you've been leading a small group that seems to have stalled out, or if your group appears to be excelling only at surface answers, it may be that real trust is the missing component that would take your group from going through the motions to seeing people grow in their love and knowledge of Jesus as they become more and more like him.

TRUST: HOW TO BUILD IT

"The best way to find out if you can trust somebody is to trust them." This is Ernest Hemingway's take on building trust with others. Without intending to offend Mr. Hemingway, I find this a bit Utopian. It's not likely that many people will walk into your group eager to extend trust to a room of people they've just met. In addition, some of you may be leading brand-new groups where no one knows anyone else, so you're stuck in a trust stalemate, waiting for someone to make the first move.

Trust is Contagious

This is where you come in as the leader. When it comes to building trust, your group will follow your lead. If you lead from a reserved and defensive posture without showing the authenticity and vulnerability you're asking of others, you will find that your group may feel safe, but it won't feel fruitful. It's hard to be the first to make that move, but when you do, you will find that people will be more willing to follow.

It's like that show "Wipeout" from some years back. Contestants had to make their way through an absurd obstacle course elevated ten to twenty feet above a pool of water. It was rare that anyone would make it through the course without taking a plunge into the water at least once. But there was an advantage to be had if someone went first. You could watch their approach and learn what to do and what to avoid. It's never desirable to be the first one out, but the risks taken by that person benefit the group as a whole. Leaders, I understand that in some measure you can't open up to the fullest extent with your group, but if you're not opening up at all, you will find that the group will follow your lead.

As you answer the discussion questions, are you willing to share about areas of conviction? Are you willing to talk about areas that you needed to repent of this week? Are you willing to ask your group to pray for your ongoing sanctification in these areas? As your group offers prayer requests, are yours meaningful and authentic, or are they overly safe not wanting to pull back the curtain on your struggles as a parent or your need to grow in patience toward your spouse? As you find yourself in times of trial, are you reaching out to your group for help? Are you accepting the offer of a meal train? Are you welcoming that brother's offer to come and mow your yard so you can focus on navigating the trial at hand? Or are you OK? You'll handle it; you appreciate the offer, but no thanks.

Your leadership will either invite trust and authentic transparency from those you lead or create even bigger obstacles to the open and honest dialog that I imagine you desire from your group. The first way to build trust is to offer that trust to those you lead.

Trust Is Commitment

I have found myself repeating a phrase recently, "It's easy to preach and hard to live." That's true of the next principle for building trust in our groups. We must be leaders who show up during the trials and follow up on the needs.

You've probably had the experience of sharing a prayer request and seeing people intently listen, nod their heads, write down the request, pray with you at that moment, and then never ask you about it again. You've probably also done this to others. As leaders hoping to build trust in our small groups, we must prioritize the follow-up. If someone shares a request that they've got a doctor's appointment this week that they're nervous about. Yes, pray for that person during your group time, but make a note, set a reminder, and have Siri remind you to follow up with them after that appointment. You have a group member who has a big interview for a potential promotion. Yes, pray for that person during your group time, but make that note, set that reminder, and tell Siri to remind you to follow up with them after that interview. It may not seem like much, but those little touches communicate that you care about your group members, that you love them, and think about them outside of the group time. This will help foster the trust that we're seeking.

Showing up is harder. Follow-up is hard because we get busy and distracted. Showing up is hard because it means sacrifice. You've got someone in your group in the hospital? Yes, mobilize the prayer line in the group and get the meal train going, but then reach out and ask them when you can visit. You've got a couple who just welcomed a baby? Yes, get them something from their registry, but then call and find a time to come and say congratulations in person. You've got someone in your group who has withdrawn and won't respond to texts or phone calls. Yes, pray for them, but maybe you should get in the car, drive to their house, and knock on their door because you want them to know that you care and that they are loved. You've got a family whose son is playing in a big game this week; yes, show the care to be interested, but also look at your calendar and show up to the game if you're available.

Don't underestimate the power of your presence as the group leader in helping to build trust among your group members. Whether it's your physical presence or your verbal presence by following up on prayer requests, these are ways to demonstrate to your people that you care about them, that they matter to you, and that they can trust you.

Trust is Communal

Have you ever considered how a desire for community seems to be universal? To put it another way, left to ourselves mankind will naturally form communities or tribes. To be sure, some of this is due to survival instinct. You stand a better chance against an enemy when you have a tribe than if you were to face that same enemy alone. But there's something more to it than that. We're created for community, which implies, at least to an extent, that we are created to trust others.

In Genesis 1:26, God declared, "Let us make man in our image, after our likeness..." We often think about what comes next: "Let them have dominion over the fish of the sea and over the birds of the heavens and over the livestock and over all the earth and over every creeping thing that creeps on the earth." So we talk of dominion, authority, and creativity, among other traits, as the primary ways we reflect the image of our Creator. But what about community? Returning to the beginning of verse 26, we find the Triune God. "Let us..." More foundational and fundamental to man's inherent need for community than our desire to survive is this concept that we were created in the image of a Trinitarian God. The Father, Son, and Holy Spirit exist in perfect communion with one another, and it is this trait woven into the fabric of our created being that prompts us to continually seek community.

The point is that a key to building trust in your small group is capitalizing on this inherent desire for community. This means that you as the leader need to create the space and environment for this community to form. Do fun things together as a group! Have potlucks, go to a baseball game, plan a progressive dinner, go look at Christmas lights together, play on the same team for a golf tournament, sponsor a table at a banquet or a conference where you can all sit together. These are all ways that you can foster community within your group. If you can create an environment within your group where people look forward to being together, you will find that a deepening trust is not far behind. As important as the regular rhythm of your normal small group routine is, this community-building aspect is equally necessary. And, what's more, there will be a symbiotic relationship between the two.

The greater sense of community you build, the richer your discussions and prayer time will be, which will, in turn, create a greater desire to be together as a community.

TRUST: WHAT TO DO WHEN IT'S BROKEN

Our dog needed to be housebroken when he first came to live with us. Initially, you understand that a puppy will have an occasional accident. Still, there comes a point at which discipline needs to be applied to curb the behavior of using the couch like a fire hydrant. When that happens, the dog understands it did wrong and will shy away from the one who disciplined him for fear of being punished again. This is the wounded puppy complex, and it can manifest in our small groups in the area of trust.

You may have someone in your group who has been a part of a small group, invested in the community, and extended trust to other people only to have that trust broken. Now, they come into your group timid, reserved, and hesitant to trust again. How do you, as the leader, help them rebuild that trust?

First, realize it's going to take time. They won't go from wounded puppy to fully restored overnight. It will take time to draw them out and into your discussion time. Having them give a prayer request that goes deeper than surface-level issues will take time. Everything in you will want to force the issue but giving them that time is essential.

Second, realize it will take more than the small group meetings. This person will need your attention and time outside of the regular meeting time. Schedule a coffee or a lunch with them. Ask them about their story. Listen, and don't feel like you need to have all the answers.

Also, don't take on a defensive posture as though they are accusing you or your group of being the same way. Getting to the heart of the issue may take several meetings, so go in knowing that. But spending one-on-one time with this person will convey that you care and that they can truly trust you. A compliment to this process may be connecting them with someone in the group you notice they gravitate towards during the meeting. Encourage that group member to pursue them as well.

Finally, identify with their wounds. We've all been betrayed and had our trust broken, and we all know how hard it is to return from that. You need to be ready to come alongside them to help them by sharing how God helped you work through the hurt and get back to trusting again. Remind them of the good blessings that come with an authentic and transparent community. And encourage them to pray that God will help them to move on and trust again.

THREATS TO TRUST

My guess is your front door has at least one lock on it and that you use that lock every day. Why? Because you care about the safety of your home. As the leader of your small group, you are expected to care about your group's safety as well. Here are some threats to building trust that need our attention.

Gossip

The prayer requests, comments, and questions shared during the small group time are for the small group, not the school carpool line or the water cooler at work. Nothing will undermine trust in a group faster than finding out someone has been talking about another group member behind their back. Even if we practice "Christian gossip" by couching it in a prayer request, it will damage the group's willingness to trust one another.

Conflict

If a group is together long enough, conflict will inevitably arise. This is especially true in the context of a community where we are ideally "doing life" with one another in such proximity. Having conflict isn't the threat; it's what we do with the conflict that is the threat. Make sure you talk to your group about conflict and conflict resolution. Have them read a book like Ken Sande's *The Peacemaker*. Offer to mediate conflict, if anyone feels like a third party is necessary or would be helpful. Encourage people to deal with conflict biblically to help preserve the group's unity.

Superficiality

Overcoming this is really what this whole chapter has been about, but the danger is that leading a superficial group is often easier than leading a fruitful group. If you want a group where members trust one another to the degree we've been talking about, it is going to get messy, and it is going to require a greater investment from you. When you lead a superficial group, you can keep things nice and tidy, confined to the 1–2 hours a week that you meet together. This temptation will arise but fight it and realize that the more superficial things remain, the less real impact will be made towards a trust-fueled, genuine community.

CONCLUSION

Author and business guru Stephen Covey called trust "the glue of life." Companies will talk about wanting to earn your trust. One doesn't have to be a Christian to understand why trust matters. It builds bridges, creates repeat business, gives people a sense of confidence in a product, and produces unpaid brand ambassadors who will tell everyone they know about their experience with _____. Trust is essential in the world in which we live. But, when it comes to your small group, trust is undeniably imperative to the overall health and function of the group. Without it, you'll never see the results you're after.

If you've been leading a group for a while and are struggling to build trust, I pray this chapter has encouraged you to think through new approaches to help change that. If you're leading a group that is thriving in this area, I pray that this chapter has encouraged you in what you are doing. Regardless of where your group is at, know that as the leader, you play an enormous role in creating trust within this community. It's a big task, but it's worth it in the end.

Keeping the Church Small

Chapter 6

HOLDING EACH OTHER ACCOUNTABLE

Pursuing Holiness with Those in Your Small Group

Mike Elliott

Sermon-based small groups are an effective tool in shepherding people by the power of God's word. Rich discussion and application of biblical text will mold the church into a sanctified body. However, outside of the group time each member will face different temptations, are at different levels of maturity, and are at the same time called to grow in their holiness (Heb. 12:14). This is where accountability can play a significant role in the life of a small group. Christians carrying out the mandates of the New Testament by confessing to one another, admonishing one another, and serving one another in the context of accountability will strengthen and unify the members of the small group.

ACCOUNTABILITY GROUPS

The topic of accountability is not discussed with much excitement in the church today. Those who speak disparagingly about it usually base their opinion on a "traumatic" experience they had, rather than what the word of God would say on the topic. It is true that the term "accountability group" will not be found in a subject index of the Bible, but the concept is found throughout the Scriptures. Christians getting together to fight sin and promote holiness is a necessity for building unity and effectiveness in the Church (see Col. 3:1–17).

However, due to the individualistic mindset that has seeped into the church, it has become clear that people do not like accountability because it implies responsibility, and nobody wants to be held liable. The church should not conform to the world's standards (Rom. 12:1-2), but instead should help Christians take ownership of the call to "walk in a manner worthy of the Lord" (Phil. 1:27), this is a vital need in every small group. What follows is a pattern for accountability that will bring God the glory he deserves, as his children try to discern what is pleasing to him (Eph. 5:8–10).

Purpose

For accountability to be effective in a small group, its purpose must be clear. The reason why group members should be involved in a partnership like this is the call in the New Testament to Christlikeness. People do not stagger into mimicking their Savior. It takes deliberate, focused, and concentrated effort, striving by the Spirit of God with other children of God to become more like the Son of God. Christians must work towards the goal for which God predestined them;

conformity to Jesus Christ (Rom. 8:29).

Approaches that seek to do this individually or in isolation are doomed to fail. Proverbs identifies the result of a secluded lifestyle, "Whoever isolates himself seeks his own desire, he breaks out against all sound judgment" (Prov. 18:1). The isolated person is a selfish person, and selfish people have no hope of becoming like Christ, who is the epitome of selflessness (Mark 10:45; Phil. 2:5–11). It is imperative to have other brothers and sisters who want to help, fight, pray, and walk alongside each other in this pursuit of Christlikeness.

Each person involved in the accountability of the group must keep the goal in mind to stop drifting into one of two extremes. The first is a group that only deals with sin. Often this becomes the focus of accountability. At best this can get someone to stop their sinful ways (an important but insufficient method of accountability) and at worst it can turn them into having a catholic confession mentality.

The other extreme would be to never confront sin but only encourage positive steps to improve certain areas of everyday life and ministry. The potential danger here is pursuing only exterior change—like rearranging the deck chairs on the Titanic—leaving the damage of the iceberg unattended and ignored because the surface look "needed" a makeover. Christians cannot "put on Christlikeness" until the gaping hole left by sin has been repaired through repentance. Outward reformation is only a facade unless there has been an internal change.

The author of Hebrews rightly exhorted his readers to have this dual mindset when pursuing *sanctification* (a theological word for Christlikeness). First, he warned them that they needed to be challenged daily by one another to make sure that sin could not deceive—robbing sin of its potency (Heb. 3:13). Then, he made sure they were "irritating" one another toward love and good works (10:24–25). This paradigm would allow the audience to lay aside the sin that entangled them and run with endurance, fixing their eyes on Christ (12:1–2). This is Christian accountability.

The Right Expectation Before Implementation

Heath Lambert has written a helpful book on combating impurity entitled Finally Free in which he gives 7 principles that will help keep a small group's expectations in line with the usage of accountability between members. Tim Challies has summarized the principles and added clarification in this helpful chart.[10]

	Accountability Is…	Accountability Is Not…
1) Effective accountability does not rely exclusively on accountability.	…one weapon among many.	…the only weapon in the fight against sin.
2) Effective accountability is involved early rather than late.	…calling out for help in the moment of temptation and before you sin.	…delayed confession—the regular reporting of sins already committed.
3) Effective accountability involves someone with maturity.	…able to function best when it occurs under the leadership of someone who has a track record of victory over the sin in question.	…going to work well if you are seeking accountability with someone who is struggling and sinning in the same area as you.
4) Effective accountability involves someone with authority (Heb. 13:17).	…involving those who can speak with authority. It may also involve those who "…watch over you as those who must give an account."	…fighting on your own; by definition, accountability is not a solo effort.

5) Effective accountability should avoid explicit details (Eph. 5:11-12).	...describing sin and temptation in general terms with the goal of enabling your accountability person to help you best.	...not a place where explicit details are shared; we must avoid fueling further temptation.
6) Effective accountability places the responsibility for confession on the person with the problem.	...full and free confession without prompting, pushing or demands for honesty.	...going repeatedly through a list of questions without making honest and up-front confession of a particular sin.
7) Effective accountability must actually hold people accountable.	...being actively involved in the life of another Christian with regular and caring communication.	...simply the commitment to meet regularly and work through a list of questions.

These principles will help the leader of the small group, as well as the participants, in administering and implementing accountability. For instance, it is helpful to note that if two people are struggling with the same sin, then it would not be wise to pair them in accountability. Also, putting the onus on the person with the problem to come and confess, rather than being asked a list of "yes" or "no" questions. But above all, it should be at the forefront of the group's mind that accountability is best implemented early, rather than after the temptation has hit. Wisely will a marine in training hear, "The more you sweat in peace, the less you bleed in war."

For the Church to succeed in its battle against Satan and his army, the greatest need is soldiers who are prepared for war. During the Revolutionary War, General George Washington led the rebels against a superior foe. One of the keys to victory was a man named Freiedrich von Stueben. He instilled discipline in the men and taught them war tactics and drills that took Washington's inexperienced men and transformed them into soldiers. He is known for taking those drills and creating a manual that was used in training combat-ready fighters in future wars. The following is designed to become like von Stueben's manual, allowing believers today to be trained in what it means to fight for God's glory as they pursue Christlikeness each day.

Putting the Horse Before the Cart

There is an old saying that goes, "Don't put the cart before the horse." It conveys the idea that if things get out of order they don't work. No cart is ever going to pull the horse. As Christians discuss accountability they must do so in the correct order. The Christian life is not begun or earned by the actions of an individual (Eph. 2:8–9). So, it would be incorrect to think that accountability is going to help someone become a Christian.

However, it would also be a mistake to assume that once a person becomes a Christian, they do not participate actively in growing to become more like Christ. Peter clarifies this for his readers in his second epistle. He makes clear that it is God who has granted believers all the things they need and has allowed them to become partakers of the divine nature (2 Pet. 1:3–4). His next statement is key, "For this very reason, make every effort to supplement your faith with virtue…" (v. 5), and the passage continues with a list of Christ-like qualities that must be worked on. Peter goes on to state that if those "qualities are yours, and are increasing, they keep you from being ineffective or unfruitful in the knowledge of our Lord Jesus Christ" (v. 8). These qualities are not to be perfect, but they cannot be stagnant either. There must be an increase, and this is where accountability will help.

To keep this focus correctly systematized in accountability, it is helpful to begin each group session with a focus on Sonship. Christians do not change to become sons of God, because they are already his children. However, the believer not only rejoices that he is called a son (1 John 3:1–3), but also embraces the responsibility that is tied to sonship (3:4–10). When there is a lack of growth or sin, discipline from the Father will follow (Heb. 12:5–11), but the ultimate desire of the child of God will always be to imitate Christ (Eph. 5:1).

ACCOUNTABILITY CATEGORIES

The New Testament uses many metaphors to describe Christians. Each of the following sections takes a metaphor and uses it as a guideline to focus on evaluating how the race toward Christlikeness is going. While there will be some overlap within the sections, each metaphor is unique enough to be discussed separately.

Steward

During times of accountability, one focus should be on stewardship—how each person is doing at being a steward. While not discussed much in today's culture, it is a thoroughly biblical metaphor and extremely helpful. A steward in the first century was a slave given the charge of managing his master's household. As people consider this area, their focus should be on *managing God's blessings.* The Lord has given both general and specific blessings to his children and he expects them to manage these well.

One characteristic that must be true of a steward is faithfulness. Both Christ and Paul attach that idea to stewardship. In Luke 12:41–48, Jesus teaches that the life he will bless is that of a faithful steward. He describes the "faithful and wise manager" as one who remains resolved in his task, even when his master is absent. This slave is rewarded for setting aside his agenda and living instead for the master's sake.

Paul connects the importance of faithfulness regarding stewardship in his correspondence with the Corinthians. After discussing rewards in chapter three, he instructs them about his apostolic ministry, stating that he is a servant and a steward of God's mystery. What is the most important quality of a steward? "Moreover, it is required of stewards that they be found faithful" (1 Cor. 4:2). Above all else, the steward should be trustworthy.

This theme of stewardship continued to be a focus of the early church fathers, who encouraged the early Christian communities to "Labor together... as God's stewards..."[11] Why would this idea be so prevalent in early Christianity and not today? It must be because the first Christians, unlike those in the church today, correctly understood their relationship to God. There was no sense of entitlement, only an eagerness to serve. This concept of stewardship is humbling and should lead the Christian to think in terms of what he has been blessed with, rather than what he is owed (1 Cor. 4:7–8).

A small group would do well to begin to establish this category in the minds of every participant because the mindset of a steward is dedicated to carrying out his master's work. Managers in the first century were given great responsibility, but it was only to be accomplished as delineated by the owner. Christians must adopt this attitude toward supervising what God has given.

For this to be useful in accountability, each person should list the areas that God has blessed them to manage. This ranges from general (time, money, talents, etc.) to specific (husband/wife relationship, children, hobbies, etc.). With many online temptations to waste precious time checking social media, sports scores, or Pinterest accounts, small groups should make sure that each member is a good steward. The accountability relationship will be productive if the individuals are constantly evaluating their faithfulness in managing God's blessings.

Soldier

The idea that Christians are soldiers and involved in warfare is common in the Bible. Peter warns that the flesh is waging a continuous battle against believers (1 Pet. 2:11; see also Gal. 5:17). Likewise, James understands the reason conflict exists in the Church, "Is it not this, that your passions are at war within you?" (Jas. 4:1). This constant attack should be motivation for the child of God to live like the Israelites in the days of Nehemiah, with a tool in one hand and a sword in the other!

An effective soldier has certain qualities. First, he has the right mindset, as Paul told Timothy, "No soldier gets entangled in civilian pursuits, since his aim is to please the one who enlisted him" (2 Tim. 2:4). It is imperative to begin with the right goal or mindset to have successful accountability. It is not enough just to stop a behavior without the proper mindset of pleasing God. Make sure that honest evaluation and drastic steps are taken to get away from sin and temptation, but do it with the desire to please God (Rom. 13:14).

Second, the effective soldier fights with the right weapon. In detailing the equipment of a soldier, Paul lists only one offensive weapon, "...the Sword of the Spirit, which is the Word of God..." (Eph. 6:17). There will be no victory over sin unless the Christian wields the

Sword of the Spirit! The Psalmist knew this truth, "I have stored up your word in my heart, that I might not sin against you" (Ps. 119:11). During times of accountability, finding Scriptures to help in the battle against sin is crucial. These verses should then be discussed, memorized, prayed through, and applied in order to win the battle.

Finally, the effective soldier wars against sin with others. His unity with other Christians strengthens his resolve, heightens his awareness, and provides the support necessary to combat sin effectively. A believer should never think so individualistically about his battle against sin that he leaves others vulnerable to attack. One reason the rebels were able to defeat a far superior army was that they stopped thinking as individual colonies and began to think as a unified nation. Patrick Henry stated, "The distinctions between Virginians, Pennsylvanians, New Yorkers, and New Englanders are no more. I am not a Virginian; I am an American!"[12] The early settlers understood an attack on any one colony was an attack on them all. During accountability, it is time to think corporately about how to fight sin. The writer of Hebrews thought this way, "...exhort one another every day, as long as it is called 'today,' that none of you may be hardened by the deceitfulness of sin" (Heb. 3:13).

Accountability partners who don't take the time to learn how to fight, hate, and kill sin will not prosper. Christians must put to death what is earthly in them (Col. 3:5) by the power of the Spirit of God (Rom. 8:13). This process will be difficult at times and requires strenuous effort. Like C.S. Lewis said, "It is something much harder than merely eating humble pie... It means killing part of yourself, undergoing a kind of death."[13] Group leaders should make sure time and effort are put into this fight against sin. It is a matter of life and death. But the joy and peace that are found on the other side of these battles are worth the struggle.

Servant

Each person who has been baptized into the Body of Christ has been given a gift to serve the Church. Paul stresses this in 1 Corinthians 12:7 where he says that each Christian has been given a gift for the common good. Peter takes this thought one step further as he states that gifts are given to serve one another and so that God may be glorified through them (1 Pet. 4:10–11). A key aspect of accountability is making sure that service to the church is taking place.

An important component of service is understanding that sacrifice will be involved. To serve involves giving up individual needs, desires, and comfort to help others. The more someone sacrifices, the more they will experience the sanctifying effect of service. People who choose not to serve God and others will become enslaved to their own desires. It is no coincidence that Paul constantly chides the Corinthian church to serve, love, and consider others in the body. Because of their lack of concern for God's glory and the good of others, their appetites controlled them. Service is non-negotiable in the Christian life.

It takes accountability to help develop this servant mindset that looks to the needs of others (Phil. 2:3–4). Dan Cathy, son of Chick-fil-A CEO Truett Cathy, notes that it took his team ten years of training to get teen employees to switch from saying "no problem" to "my pleasure" when responding to a customer. But that selfless point of view is what gets them such high ratings in Zagat and Consumer Reports.[14] The leader of the small group should make sure that their members adopt this mindset in the church.

While it is crucial to evaluate giftedness, effectiveness, and the joy of service, it is imperative that believers make themselves available and teachable. A readiness and willingness to serve, combined with a teachable attitude, will go far in the kingdom of God. Groups should monitor how open and moldable they are in the area of service. Each person should have a ministry post in which they are serving. The people who aren't ministering usually suffer from one of two forms of pride—self-pity, or self-promotion—and those need to be addressed in an accountability meeting.

Paul warned against both of these manifestations of pride in 1 Corinthians 12:14–25. Regarding the idea that the service rendered is either meaningless or not good enough (self-pity), Paul states that God has sovereignly designed the body so that every piece serves a purpose. This would at the same time stop someone with a more visible gift from promoting their service as more important than others (self-promotion). The various gifts of service should never be used in competition, but rather in concert with one another.

The ambition of a servant must be the same as Paul taught the Corinthians, "Strive to excel in building up the church" (1 Cor. 14:12). Complacency is corrosive and will rob God of the glory he deserves and hinder others from being served. Those who have served in areas of the church for an extended period of time could suffer from this damaging disposition. Accountability partners should be encouraging and challenging one another to grow in their abilities and to overcome plateaus of apathy in their service.

Student

Every Christian is a disciple and that means that every Christian is a learner. Each person must realize that it is not if they will be a theologian, but what kind of theologian they will be. The more repetition, understanding, and discipline in reading the Bible that believers have the more they will be prepared to do what God has called them to do. Ignorance of biblical truth will lead to immature thinking. Children of God must avoid apathy in their pursuit of knowing God.

This area of accountability focuses on the importance of growing in our understanding of God. Paul prayed that the Colossians would increase in their knowledge of God (1:10). Jeremiah reminded the Israelites that nothing was more important than understanding and knowing the God of the universe (9:23–24). And like studying for any discipline, this takes hard work. Some key ways to grow in this knowledge are by memorizing and meditating on Scripture, discussing and applying sermons, and independent systematic studies of central doctrines. Other resources should be used as supplements, but never take supremacy over the scriptures themselves.

Disastrous consequences follow those who choose not to study the Bible. Hebrews 5:11–14 paints a vivid warning for those who choose not to grow in their knowledge of God's Word. The writer desired to share glorious truths about Christ but the people had become "dull of hearing." This phrase indicates the laziness that hindered the growth of these people, leading them to be "unskilled in the word of righteousness." Unfamiliarity and apathy must be confronted in accountability. We need the courage to speak in the way Paul did to the Corinthians, " Wake up from your drunken stupor, as is right, and do not go on sinning. For some have no knowledge of God." (1 Cor. 15:34).

The application of the Bible is key. A good student is not just one who knows a lot, but one who uses that information to build up others (1 Cor. 8:1). Encouragement to keep up spiritual disciplines such as Bible reading and memorization should take place during group accountability time. People in a small group would do well to also hold one another accountable in reading certain books on Christian living and theology. Again, these must supplement, not supplant, God's Word.

To study the Word of God this way takes dedication and discipline. As a nineteen-year-old young man, Jonathan Edwards penned his famous resolutions. His thinking is needed today: "Resolved, to study the Scriptures so steadily, constantly, and frequently that I may find, and plainly perceive myself to grow in the knowledge of them."[15]

CONCLUSION

Free soloing is a type of rock climbing that involves only one person and the rock they are scaling. No ropes. No spotter. The climber faces off against the mountain. As one can imagine, this type of recreation is extremely dangerous and can have deadly consequences. Sadly, it is not much different from the way some people in small groups approach the Christian life. They refuse the help of others and choose to struggle against sin alone, quickly finding that deadly consequences are associated with their choice.

King David was a man after God's own heart, but he had a season in his life where he isolated himself and plunged headfirst into sin (see

2 Sam. 11). And it took the rebuke of a friend/prophet to get him to confess his sins. Who knows what would have happened had David gone to Nathan first and revealed his temptations? Knowing how faithful and bold Nathan was, it seems that those sins would have been put to death. Small group accountability should function in such a way that no person lives his or her life like a free solo climber. A mutual love for God and one another should cause believers to race toward Christlikeness together.

The young Scottish pastor Robert Murray M'Cheyne had the right outlook on ministry when he said, "It is not great talents God blesses so much as great likeness to Jesus."[16] When accountability in small groups has the singular focus of growing to be like Christ, great things will happen for the church. This should be the desire of all Christians; that the universal church would grow to "mature manhood, to the measure of the stature of the fullness of Christ" (Eph. 4:13).

Chapter 7

DISCIPLESHIP IN SMALL GROUPS

Making Mature Followers of Jesus

Bruce Blakey

Small groups in the church provide a virtual greenhouse for practicing disciple-making. Because of the shared commitments of the group and the time spent together, relationships are formed and deepened, which enhances the goal of the small group—true discipleship.

Unfortunately, as Leroy Eims pointed out decades ago in his book, *The Lost Art of Disciple Making*, most people in the church do not understand what the terms discipleship and disciple-making even mean. This is a tragedy of major proportions because disciple-making is the mission that the Lord Jesus has given to the church.

I was fortunate because the man who led me to the Lord met with me almost every day for three months and modeled what disciple-making looked like. Shortly after that, I was introduced to small group ministries, and I was exposed to what disciple-making looks like in that context as well. Additionally, I was eventually given the opportunity to disciple people individually and in a small group setting, gaining valuable ministry experience.

My initial experience with disciple-making was in a campus parachurch ministry, and I had not seen how this process worked within the context of the local church. Since then, I have been able to practice disciple-making within the church and see the value that this context adds to the ministry. In my years of lay ministry while working for a bank, and now in my thirty-three years of pastoral ministry, I have had numerous opportunities to both practice individual disciple-making and implement disciple-making ministries.

However, to this day, the biggest obstacle to disciple-making in the church is that most people do not really know what it is. They have not been taught about it, they have not seen it modeled, and they have not really been discipled themselves. Therefore, this chapter will need to begin with defining what we mean by discipleship.

DISCIPLESHIP DEFINED

A simple definition: *disciple-making is the process by which a person goes from being an unbeliever to a mature follower of Jesus Christ.* This all happens through (1) evangelizing—the presentation and reception of the gospel message; (2) edifying—being taught the truth of the word and the application of it; and (3) equipping—training the disciple to make more disciples. These goals of disciple-making give clear direction to a ministry and make all the ministries of the church complementary rather than competitive.

To many people, being a Christian means: "I believe in Jesus and I go to church; in church, I will listen to the sermons; I might sing during the "worship" time; I might get involved in some kind of a fellowship group; I might volunteer to serve in some ministry; I might give some money; and I might even invite someone to church." But what is missing is a clear understanding of what it is all about.

As Mike Fabarez has said in *Partners*, the church is a disciple-making organization.[17] Certainly, our enemy, the devil, understands this and he will use every tool at his disposal to get the church off track. We must be resolved in our commitment to disciple-making.

The church must be intentional to provide opportunities for people to be involved in something smaller than the main service. The leaders of these small groups must lead the group with the goal of seeing everyone mature in their relationship with Christ. Some members of the group may need evangelizing and while evangelism should not occupy the small group time, it must be pursued outside of the group with the individual.

All the believers in the group need edifying—to be built up and encouraged to learn and apply the truth of God's word. The leaders must work to make small group times conform to this objective and provide additional times (perhaps separate men's and women's meetings) to accomplish this goal. As the leader builds relationships with the small group members, one-on-one opportunities will present themselves. It is during these times that a leader can personally help the believer grow in his or her walk with the Lord. Many times, counseling opportunities will also arise in these relationships, here the leader can provide biblical counsel regarding marriage, a particular sin problem, or a challenging circumstance that the group member is facing.

Equipping can also take place in the small group. For example, after a leader goes through a one-on-one discipleship program like *Partners* with someone in the group, he can encourage this group member to take another member of the group through the program. The leader can also provide opportunities for others to help lead the group. By doing this kind of intentional equipping, the leader is beginning to multiply his ministry.

All of this should help us to see that serious equipping and training are required to produce leaders who can effectively lead a disciple-making small group. There is a big difference between leading a social, friendly, and even somewhat helpful small group and leading a group that is really discipleship oriented.

THE VALUE OF DISCIPLESHIP

To see the importance of discipleship and be more motivated to pursue it, we need to fully appreciate its value. We can consider the value from 5 perspectives.[18]

The Value to Christ

Christ placed a great emphasis on discipleship during his earthly ministry. Jesus had a small group of twelve men. Out of those twelve, he invested more time into three of them (Peter, James, and John) and even more time into one of them (Peter). Men were his method (Mark 3:14). After his resurrection, Jesus commanded his disciples to do what he had done (Matt. 28:20) and they did (2 Tim. 2:2). This was the Master Plan, and we are to continue the pattern.

The Value to the Disciple

Many Christians stay spiritually immature for many years because no one takes an interest in their growth in Christ. No one helps them advance. They have no one to come alongside them and disciple them. Those who are more mature should care for the less mature (Titus 2 – older to younger women; older to younger men). This pattern produces specific benefits:

- Increases the Rate of Growth

  The disciple is taught to study the Bible and pray, and to keep his focus on the Person of Christ. He has an example in the discipler of what it looks like to live the Christian life (2 Tim. 3:10).

- Stops Wrong Behavior Patterns

  The disciple is helped with putting off and putting on specific practices. The discipler provides necessary correction and acts like a good coach to the new disciple.

- Provides Protection from the Enemy

  The disciple has limited biblical understanding and discernment and can be easily tempted or led astray. The more mature discipler can help warn and instruct the new disciple and direct him away from sin.

- Provides Friendship/Fellowship

  The new disciple is not isolated or alone and has someone to talk with and pray with.

- Provides Counsel

The disciple can be helped with decisions he is facing, learning to evaluate them biblically.

- Equipping Takes Place

The disciple is given a framework for living the Christian life, so he can then disciple others.

Many Christians miss out on these significant benefits because there is little commitment to discipleship.

The Value to the Discipler

There is great joy in successfully discipling others (3 John 4; 1 Thess. 2:9–10; 3:9). It doesn't always work out the way you want, and it is not always a delight. But there are always great benefits:

- Purifies the Life of the Discipler

You will become aware of your weaknesses and will have greater accountability to keep your life above reproach. You will be questioned about practical things – movies, TV, music, schooling of children, etc. They will look to you for an example as to how to live as a Christian.

- Develops Ministry Skills

You will learn to teach, to counsel, and to guide by doing it. And your involvement with your disciple will greatly inform the rest of your ministry. Over time, as you gain knowledge and sharpen your skills by discipling others you will become more and more effective for Christ, the church, and in your small group.

- Provides a Necessary Outlet

Discipling others prevents the sit, soak, and sour syndrome that is all too common in our churches. It keeps the fire burning. It is the best way to multiply your ministry and your impact. As a discipler you must continue to grow in your relationship with God and be available not just to hang out, but for the great purpose of discipling and equipping others.

The Value to the Church

A commitment to discipling strengthens the church by producing workers and developing leaders. We see this pattern in Ephesians 4:11–12. Leaders in the church are to build up and train the rest for the work of ministry. The work is for all but all need training. Bible teaching and ministries that equip believers in the word of God are important, but we cannot stop there. The church needs to multiply disciples.

If the church is to continue in future generations as a strong, dynamic, working fellowship of believers that adhere to the truth of Scripture, then the ministry of discipling and presenting every man (including children and youth) complete in Christ, is absolutely essential (Col. 1:28).

This is one reason why small groups, where real fellowship is promoted and genuine discipleship is practiced, are so important to the ongoing life and growth of the church.

We cannot just have programs. We cannot just have small groups that discuss the Bible. We must include the personal element of disciple-making.

The Value to the World

Jesus said to make disciples of all nations. Discipleship begins with evangelism. A commitment to discipleship pushes believers to evangelize and equips them to do it effectively. Mature disciples will have an impact on the world.

Some reasons the church makes little impact today is because many Christians are weak and confused, too self-righteous, or too fearful and isolated. True discipleship equips and propels us out into the world that needs the message of the Good News. We must have a heart for people. We need an inward motivation to fellowship with Christ and an outward motivation to become witnesses for Christ. True disciple-making will develop this within a church and this kind of a church will make an impact and penetrate the community with the gospel.

Many might think that successful discipleship requires certain skills, which is true to a degree. Hopefully, the necessary skills will be passed on in the equipping stage of the training. The Bible, however, would point to something else as the most important feature in a discipler/small group leader's life and that is the example they set.

THE IMPORTANCE OF EXAMPLE

I have often heard it said that spiritual leadership can be summed up in one word—example. Leaders must provide an example in both precept (what they say) and practice (how they live) understanding that their life is the most powerful message.

Again, I think it will be helpful to break this down and examine the importance of being an example from three perspectives.

The Importance of Example as Seen in Scripture

The Apostle Paul was a master disciple maker. In his letters, he emphasized being an example and following an example.

In 1 Corinthians 4:16, Paul tells his spiritual children in Corinth to be imitators of him. The Greek word translated imitate is the word from which we get mimic. This presents a vivid picture of what it is to follow someone's example. The amazing thing about this reference is the context. In the next verse, Paul tells the Corinthians that because he wants them to imitate him, he is sending Timothy to them. He says of Timothy that he is "my beloved and faithful child in the Lord" and he will "remind you of my ways in Christ (v. 17)." At first, this might sound confusing. Paul wants the Corinthians to imitate him but is sending Timothy to them. Paul had so thoroughly discipled Timothy that having Timothy with them was like having Paul himself.

Paul was not setting himself up as the ultimate example. Only Christ can be that. However, he called others to follow his example as he followed Christ (1 Cor. 11:1). Paul consistently called on others to follow his example and the example of other faithful Christians. "Brothers, join in imitating me, and keep your eyes on those who walk according to the example you have in us" (Phil. 3:17).

Paul urged leaders like Timothy (1 Tim. 4:12) and Titus (Titus 2:7) to set an example for those they led. It is impossible to read Paul's letters without seeing his emphasis on example.

Other New Testament writers emphasize this as well (Heb. 6:12; 13:7; 1 Pet. 5:1–4). 3 John 11 says, "Beloved, do not imitate evil but imitate good," and in his letter John points to the good example of Demetrius and the evil example of Diotrophes.

The New Testament mandate for modeling is clear. It should develop in us as small group leaders a genuine humility and a renewed dependence upon the Lord and his resources, looking to him as the ultimate model (John 13:15; Eph. 5:1; 1 John 2:6; Phil. 2:5).

Discipling begins with the lifestyle of the discipler. The Bible never tells us to imitate an abstraction. One of the primary responsibilities of a small group leader is to set a godly example. Your example is crucial. You must have a life that is worth emulating.

Having briefly looked at the importance that Scripture places on example, let's consider the practical value of setting an example in discipleship.

The Importance of Example to the Disciple

In a day when we value style over substance, we tend to downplay the importance of setting an example. However, the effect of a godly life is powerful and should never be underestimated. This is also encouraging, because I may never have the style that people are looking for, but I can, by God's help, develop a godly lifestyle. And, when it comes to spiritual impact, it is not so much instruction that causes change as it is the example we set. Just think of the way children mimic their parents.

To the unconverted or the young untaught believer, a godly life is somewhat foreign. They need to see an example of the real thing. Think of some ways a young believer may be helped by the godly example of another believer:

- They can be encouraged by the growth they see in others.

Knowing that the person they are watching didn't always live like this, and seeing how they have grown and changed provides hope and helps the young believer not to grow weary.

- The young believer can learn what it is to follow the Lord by following the Lord's people. The untaught believer can gain practical help in how to apply God's word to everyday life. Christ's pattern of living can be found in his people and this is a tremendous help to a young believer.

- The steadfast example of a mature believer can help the young believer to overcome fear. Paul's faithful, bold witness while in prison in Rome provided encouragement to many believers who would have otherwise been fearful (Phil. 1:14).

The value of having an example to follow for the young believer is obvious. But there is also great value to the discipler in having a consistent example.

The Importance of Example to the Discipler

The issue from the perspective of the discipler is one of credibility. To lead a small group with credibility, you must be a godly example.

Your life as the leader is an open exhibit. Your life will either prove or invalidate your spoken words. As Paul told Timothy, how he lives before others will determine his credibility (1 Tim 4:12). Timothy was to gain the respect of others by living a godly life. Gaining the respect of others is not secured by reminding them of your position nor by telling them what to do, it is through living a consistent life of biblical integrity.

Do people respect you? Do you have credibility with others? One of the primary responsibilities of a discipler is to set a godly example.

You must teach and live the truth; expound and exemplify the truth; talk and walk the truth; explain and exhibit the truth; lead by precept and practice; lead by lip and life; and any other way you want to describe it.

Being an example is quite a responsibility. Much of the direction a church will take is determined by the models of its small group leaders. It is imperative, therefore, that they be models worthy of following because, as our Lord said, "Everyone when he is fully trained will be like his teacher" (Luke 6:40).

Here are some specific, critical ways that the discipler should provide an example:

- Love for the Lord Jesus Christ

This is the supreme priority. When Jesus restored Peter to his ministry after the resurrection, he asked Peter three times if he loved him (John 21:15–17).

- Love for People

We would all do well to take note of Paul's love for the people he ministered to (For example, see Phil. 1:7, 8, 24–25; 4:1).

- Commitment to Ministry

You must be willing to count the cost. Being an effective disciple-maker takes time, emotional stamina, physical strength, and financial sacrifice, as well as making you aware of your inadequacies.

- Student of the Bible

Along with teaching the disciple how to study the Bible, the discipler must model the application and study of God's word in his or her own life, as the disciple must learn how to rightly interpret and apply God's word.

- Consistent Prayer Life

The disciple-maker needs to demonstrate a genuine prayer life for the disciple in the hope that he will receive the same request that the disciples made of Jesus, "Lord, teach us to pray" (Luke 11:1).

- Godly Marriage and Family

Undoubtedly this is the one area where the disciple-maker will provide much counsel. Therefore, the discipler must know what the Bible teaches and faithfully apply these truths and principles in his or her marriage and family. When we help the disciple in marriage and family we are potentially affecting generations to come—this is exactly what we want in making disciples.

- Living for God's Glory

It should be evident that our supreme goal and our source of true motivation is to honor, please, and glorify our Lord.

Having briefly looked at what disciple-making is, the value of disciple-making, and the importance of the example of the disciple-maker, let's conclude by turning our attention to the goals of disciple-making.

THE GOALS OF DISCIPLE MAKING

It is important to know what we are aiming at. When a church looks at its small group and disciple-making ministries, the goals must be known, so that there can be clarity and a means of evaluation. Here are three essential goals we should strive for.

Disciples Who Are Mature (Col. 1:28)

We want disciples who are fully developed and spiritually mature. This means:

- They are Christlike in their character (Eph. 4:13).

- They are very motivated to live in a way that is pleasing to the Lord (2 Cor. 5:14).

- They have a consistent walk. The direction of their life is one of growth (Phil. 3:14).

- They have stability in their life due to a clear understanding of biblical truth (Eph. 4:14).

- Their life testimony is above reproach. They are blameless in their behavior (Phil. 2:15; 1 Tim. 3:2).

Disciples Who Are Serving (Eph. 4:16)

We want disciples who are actively involved in serving and understand the centrality of the local church. In other words:

- They are enthusiastically involved in the life of the church (Acts 4:12).

- They are using their gifts to serve the church (Rom. 12:3–8; 1 Cor. 12).

- They are fulfilling the ministry God has designed for them (1 Pet. 4:10–11).

- They are actively participating in the fellowship of the church (Heb. 10:24–25). They are fulfilling the "one anothers" within the fellowship.

Disciples Who Are Multipliers (Matt. 28:19–20)

We want disciples who will multiply themselves by making more disciples. In 1 Thessalonians 1:6–8, we see that Paul, Silvanus, and Timothy made disciples of some Thessalonians who followed their example and became examples for the believers in Macedonia and Achaia. This is how a ministry grows and multiplies.

To sum up, a multiplying disciple is someone who knows how to evangelize and does it faithfully. They know how to help others grow in their faith and they intentionally pursue opportunities to do this. And, the multiplying disciple can equip others to reproduce themselves.

This summary takes us back to our beginning definition of discipleship. It is as simple as following the commission and example of our Lord.

CONCLUSION

We must have an emphasis on the word of God and practice genuine fellowship within our small groups. But we cannot stop there. If we are to be faithful to our Lord, we must practice true discipleship. The leader must commit to making disciples. He must be purposefully working towards the maturity of each person in the group. This will guide the group times and also include personal discipleship. As leaders, we may not be able to meet with everyone individually, but we can meet with someone. We just need to get started and stay committed.

I think back to the man who led me to Christ and discipled me, and all that has come from that investment. A few years ago, we had the opportunity to get together and reminisce about all the Lord has done. What has happened is far beyond what we could have imagined, but it bears testimony to the effectiveness of the Master's plan.

It is amazing to consider what the Lord can do with one faithful disciple. In closing, here is a story that should encourage us all.

> One remarkable example of multiplication in action is the story of Dawson Trotman, founder of the Navigators, and Les Spencer, a navy man. After Trotman had been teaching Spencer truths from God's Word for some time, Spencer brought a friend from his ship to Trotman and said, "Dawson, I want you to teach him all you have taught me."
>
> But Dawson said, "I am not going to teach him, you are going to teach him. If you cannot teach him what I have taught you, then I have failed."

Les Spencer began to teach his friend, and the multiplication process began. Spencer's friend eventually found someone else who needed to be taught, and the process continued until one hundred twenty-five men were meeting every week for prayer and Bible study on the ship. Those men then went to other ships and bases until, at the height of World War II, there were groups of believers on over one thousand ships and naval bases all over the world.

Do you know what happened? The FBI heard about those groups with no name or charter and began to investigate. When the agents asked a person how the group got started, the reply was, "I do not know. I met someone on another ship who started a group." So, the FBI agents went to that person with their question only to be referred to another person on another ship. The investigation continued for three months until they were finally able to trace the whole ministry back to Dawson Trotman. That is how the Navigators got started. That is multiplication![19]

Instead of this happening on ships, imagine what it would be like if this were happening in churches. Imagine if this was happening in your church!

Chapter 8

CARING WELL FOR THOSE IN YOUR SMALL GROUP

A Step-By-Step Approach

Kellen Allen

In Ecclesiastes 3:1–8 we are reminded that this life is full of ups and downs, as the author gives us fourteen couplets about the seasons of life. These truths should remind us that there will inevitably be seasons where you or someone within your small group will need care and support to get through a current trial. Being able to care for those in need prayerfully and practically is one of the biggest blessings and examples of the love of Christ that one can provide. Here is a step-by-step approach to how you can be a great blessing by caring for those in need!

CONNECTION

Reaching Out Right Away

Often, within a small group, when someone is going through a trial, the default assumption is to think someone else is probably going to reach out to the one in need. It is also common to feel that you do not know the person that well, so you will let someone who is more personally connected reach out. This mistake is like a blooper commonly occurring in baseball—even at the professional level. The batter hits the ball, and the ball goes straight up in the air. Everyone assumes this will be an easy routine catch-and-out. I mean these are professional baseball players, right? But, as two or three of the fielders slowly get under the ball saying, "I got it," the ball drops in the middle of them with no one catching it. It is a very embarrassing play that happens more often than you would think. Everyone assumes someone else will make the catch, but in the end, no one does. The same thing can happen when you assume others will reach out to connect with someone in need, and in the end, no one does.

If a situation arises within your small group where someone needs care, do not assume others will make the connection. Take it upon yourself to reach out right away. The person will appreciate it, and you will know that they have been well cared for. I have never heard anyone going through a trial say, "I am burdened because I have too many people reaching out to care for me." I have learned from my experience in caring for those in need that the strongest connections happen when you are there for people during challenging times. God can use your care for others during a trial to produce a lifelong connection that you may not have otherwise had.

Initially, you may have that feeling of hesitation, thinking: *What do I say? How do I offer to help? This feels odd because I barely know the person.* Continue reading, and I will provide you with some practical steps to help you with these thoughts.

Presence Is Huge

When a situation arises and there is a need, reach out right away to let the person know you are there for them and praying for them. That initial point of contact is very important, but often the best way for the one in need to really feel cared for is to experience the physical presence of others. You should ask before you show up unannounced, but in most cases, your presence will be welcomed, and you should look to go beyond the call, text, or email to be physically present whenever possible. Your physical presence is very impactful! The Book of Job contains a great example of the power of presence in times of need.

> Now when Job's three friends heard of all this evil that had come upon him, they came each from his own place, Eliphaz the Temanite, Bildad the Shuhite, and Zophar the Naamathite. They made an appointment together to come to show him sympathy and comfort him. And when they saw him from a distance, they did not recognize him. And they raised their voices and wept, and they tore their robes and sprinkled dust on their heads toward heaven. And they sat with him on the ground seven days and seven nights, and no one spoke a word to him, for they saw that his suffering was very great. (Job 2:11–13)

Notice that Job's friends simply sat with him for seven days and seven nights not saying a word. If you are familiar with the rest of the story, it may have been best if they had remained quiet, but in that moment just their presence was comforting to Job and was what he needed. Of course, speaking truth at the right time is important, but understand that just being there "says" a lot on its own.

Physically Close

When you do have the opportunity to be physically present with someone in need here are a few things to keep in mind to ensure your time spent is a blessing and not a burden. Depending on the situation, if the person is sick, grieving, or hurting in some way, a feeling of isolation and loneliness has probably already set in. This is why it is important that after physically showing up, you try to be physically close in proximity. The goal is for the person to be comforted by the fact that you are not overly concerned about the current situation and that you care most about them. For example, if someone has had a reconstructive type of surgery or is noticeably ill, and you visit them but stay on the other side of the room, how do you think that person will feel? They are probably already insecure, and now those insecurities have become a reality because they think it must be so bad that you don't even want to come close. Instead, to the best of your ability, aim to draw near to them and bring them the comfort of normalcy and care. Jesus gave us an example of this in his care and healing of Simon's mother-in-law.

> And he arose and left the synagogue and entered Simon's house. Now Simon's mother-in-law was ill with a high fever, and they appealed to

him on her behalf. And he stood over her and rebuked the fever, and it left her, and immediately she rose and began to serve them. (Luke 4:38–39)

Jesus was not concerned about the illness. He showed love, care, and compassion for Simon's mother-in-law and "stood over her." He could have healed her from afar, but instead in this situation, he went close to her in physical proximity. Of course, many factors that affect the situation cannot all be listed here, so use discernment when you arrive in person, but always be mindful that the closer you are the more comforting it can be to the one in need.

Listen, Listen, Listen

A concern for many people when visiting someone who is sick or shut-in is, "What will I say?" I hope to bring you comfort by saying that when you are making a home or hospital visit, less is more (in most situations). That is why you should go into any visit prepared to listen, listen, listen. Often, if the person you are ministering to can speak as they normally do, they will do most of the talking. And that is a good thing because as they talk you can quickly pick up on their needs.

It is always good to identify a few questions that you can ask the person you are visiting ahead of time. Ask questions regarding how the current situation came about, how it is impacting them personally and spiritually, and how you can meet any practical needs. If you do not know them well, you can ask additional questions about their family, their work, and their relationship with the Lord. Often, people feel a little timid to ask too many questions about the current situation.

However, I have found in most cases that the person is ready and willing to discuss the situation. In fact, it makes it more awkward for the one in need when it is not discussed.

Being a good listener requires you to know when you are talking too much. Don't go in prepared to preach a sermon (I will share more on what things you should focus on talking about later in this chapter). It is easy to think that if you fill the time by speaking, there will be less awkward silence. But, a little silence is okay. If you find yourself speaking more than the person in need of care, take a pause and ask open-ended questions to get yourself listening more than you are speaking. Through listening, you will learn a lot about the person and how you can best care for them in the coming days, weeks, and months.

MEETING NEEDS

Bear one another's burdens, and so fulfill the law of Christ. (Gal. 6:2)

As Christians, we are called to bear one another's burdens. That means, if someone else is hurting, we are to be by their side to go through the crisis with them, and to help them through it in the strength of the Lord. When you are truly bearing the burden with another, you are in tune with the current situation and ready and willing to help in any way you can. When it comes to meeting needs, some people will come right out and tell of the practical needs that they have, but most people will not say much initially because they do not want to feel as if they are interrupting or burdening other people. That is why you should seek to go above and beyond to meet the person's needs. For example, someone who is grieving the loss of a loved one will hear a well-intended, "Let me know if you need anything" countless times. We all say it. However, put yourself in their shoes (and maybe this has been you in the past). If the person hears that twenty-five plus times, he or she must now decide who would be least burdened by their needs and requests, and to what extent the selected person is willing to meet that need. I am sure the small-framed elderly lady wasn't thinking of moving furniture to clear out a room when she said, "Let me know if you need anything."

The better approach to meeting a need, once you have an idea of what those needs are, is to let the person know your plans. "I'm going to bring over dinner for you one day this week, what day works best for you?" That is a much easier and more helpful question to answer while trying to figure out a lot of other things. It minimizes the decisions the person must make and takes care of a need that you know they have. That small and more assertive adjustment is welcomed in just about every situation I have experienced. In the worst-case scenario, they decline that particular offer because it is already covered, and you have demonstrated that you are truly ready and willing to help if another need arises.

Meals

A great way to meet a need is by providing a meal. A meal is a helpful and practical way to care for someone. In First Kings, we see an example of the angel of the Lord doing this very thing for Elijah during one of the most challenging trials of his life.

Ahab told Jezebel all that Elijah had done, and how he had killed all the prophets with the sword. Then Jezebel sent a messenger to Elijah, saying, "So may the gods do to me and more also, if I do not make your life as the life of one of them by this time tomorrow." Then he was afraid, and he arose and ran for his life and came to Beersheba, which belongs to Judah, and left his servant there. But he himself went a day's journey into the wilderness and came and sat down under a broom tree. And he asked that he might die, saying, "It is enough; now, O Lord, take away my life, for I am no better than my fathers." And he lay down and slept under a broom tree. And behold, an angel touched him and said to him, "Arise and eat." And he looked, and behold, there was at his head a cake baked on hot stones and a jar of water. And he ate and drank and lay down again. And the angel of the Lord came again a second time and touched him and said, "Arise and eat, for the journey is too great for you." And he arose and ate and drank, and went in the strength of that food forty days and forty nights to Horeb, the mount of God. (1 Kings 19:1–8)

As seen in this passage, not only is food a blessing to the person in need of care, but it also provides strength and energy to continue on. The person must eat at some point, so initiate by asking, "I would like to bring you a meal. What day and time works best for you?"

If you know it would be beneficial for them to receive multiple meals over time, you can organize a meal support plan through www.mealtrain.com. It is a free and organized way to get others involved. You may be thinking, does it need to be a homecooked meal? Much of that depends on the time you have and the person's preferences. While a home-cooked meal adds a great personal touch, sometimes grabbing takeout from their favorite restaurant is a better option. Be sure to get an idea of what the person you are caring for likes and does not like and if they have any food allergies before making or purchasing the meal. While you may think it is the best meal on the planet, everyone may not share your love for mom's special butternut squash soup.

Besides providing meals, you can discern the person's other needs by asking, "How can I help to serve you?" It may be running an errand, babysitting, dog walking, or even being the go-between person for the one in need and someone in the church who can provide a specialty resource (e.g., auto mechanic, attorney, handyman, etc.).

COMMUNICATING

Choosing words of comfort wisely is important as you look to care for someone who is facing a trial. If you are not thoughtful in the things that you communicate your good intentions can easily go wrong. One of the first things you must think through is how well you know the person. This will determine how deep you can go, or in some cases, how firm you may need to be with them to help them through their situation.

Every situation is different. For example, consider someone who has lost a loved one. They may be tempted to isolate at first. In this situation, if you have a close relationship with the person, you could more firmly and lovingly encourage them to get to church and be in fellowship with the body of Christ. Someone who does not know them as well might try the same but it could be perceived as insensitive if not approached with more love than firmness. The same message and truth regarding the need to be around the body of Christ could be received very differently based on the established relationship.

Regardless of the relationship connection, the most important communication that needs to take place is to remind them to hope and trust in Christ! They will need to hear this repeatedly because the spiritual warfare and ongoing trial can make God's promises appear distant due to the focus on earthly pain. Trust and hope in Christ can guide a person through any situation. Job remembered God's faithfulness during the major trial of his life:

> For I know that my Redeemer lives, and at the last he will stand upon the earth. (Job 19:25)

He reminded himself of this truth and this is the hope-filled theme that we need to highlight for our friends in need. We all, especially during trials, need to be reminded that this world is not our home and that this present world was never promised to be trial-free. A good practical tip to prepare yourself for any visit is to keep a list of helpful Bible verses based on various circumstances handy. You can use these verses to encourage the person and to remind them of God's plan and his promises in tough times.

ONGOING CARE

When caring for those in need within your small group, it is often easier to remember to check in and meet needs during, or right after the person's trial. However, the loneliest times for the person are often days, weeks, or months after the initial crisis occurred. It is during this time that the impacted person is trying to transition back to normal life, but he or she no longer has the same consistent connection with others to provide prayer support and practical help.

This is where technology can be helpful. Set weekly calendar reminders for an extended period, so you remember to reach out and connect with them. Additionally, and more importantly, set yourself a reminder to continue to pray for them consistently.

Be Patient

Not everyone moves at the same pace. This is important to remember. The amount of care one person might need will differ from the next. And, the time it takes for an individual to get back to a place of normalcy in life will be different as well. It is important for you to ask questions of the person to gauge how he or she is progressing. Patience will help with transparency in conversations and will assist them in moving forward because they do not feel rushed and have been shown grace and kindness. You cannot expect people to move back to normal life as quickly as you think they should, or as you have seen others do.

A practical way to help them progress is to include them in events where they can be around other people. As mentioned previously, when going through a trial the tendency is to isolate. As someone who loves and cares for the person, you can provide great help by making sure they are in fellowship with the body of Christ.

PRAYER

The final but most important care you can provide for a person in need is to pray for them. And to make sure others are in prayer for them as well. James 5:15 tells us:

And the prayer of faith will save the one who is sick, and the Lord will raise him up. And if he has committed sins, he will be forgiven. (Jas. 5:15)

Often people will mindlessly say, "I'm praying for you, is there anything more I can do?" The answer to that specific question every time is, "No." There is absolutely nothing "more" that we can do than pray. Making our petitions known to God on behalf of the one facing a trial is the most powerful thing that we can do—because God is the all-powerful one and the only one who can truly change things. That being said, I know when most people use the phrase, they are not implying that they can give something greater than God through prayer, but it should remind us that prayer is the most important thing that we can do. And, if you are looking for a better way to phrase the above question, simply state: "I am praying for you. Are there any additional practical needs I can help with?"

It is always a great idea to ensure that your entire small group is involved in the prayer requests and updates so that the whole group can take part in praying and caring for the one in need. Prayer is powerful! And, prayer is needed, knowing that through it all God will be the one to provide peace, comfort, and strength.

CONCLUSION

Caring for someone in need will usually not come at the most convenient time, so always remember how much more God cares about us doing his will by loving others, rather than being married to our agendas. In Matthew 22, a lawyer attempts to test Jesus by asking him "Teacher, which is the great commandment in the Law?" Jesus responded "You shall love the Lord your God with all your heart and with all your soul and with all your mind. This is the great and first commandment. And a second is like it: You shall love your neighbor as yourself" (Matt. 22:36–39).

During his earthly ministry, Jesus exemplified loving God and loving others better than anyone. I am certain we can all agree that Jesus' schedule was demanding. However, throughout the Gospels, we see many examples of him pausing from what he was doing to lovingly care for someone in need. As Christ's followers, we should imitate his pattern and seek to show the love of Christ to others, knowing that God will work powerfully in a variety of ways through our caring actions. Caring for those in need will help hurting people work through their trials and fix their minds on Jesus—all because they are experiencing the love of Christ through us.

Chapter 9

PRAYING TOGETHER

A Guide for Effective Group Prayer

Mike Elliott

Commercials for new medications are plastered all over televisions across America. They share a similar format and usually begin by showing a person hunched over in pain on a dim, grey screen, while the narrator lists the symptoms. Then the name of the new medication is flashed across the television—now everything is in bright Technicolor. The person who was formerly incapacitated is now frolicking in a field with a renewed vigor for life. And just as people who suffer from those same symptoms reach for their phones, the "possible side effects" are listed. They start out innocent, headaches, or nausea, but then quickly spiral out of control to loss of vital organs and the development of a British accent! While the side effects might not be that crazy, they are still a possibility, and for most people, if they are a *possibility* then the medication is not an option.

There is a promise in Scripture, not a possibility, that God *will* oppose the proud but give grace to the humble (Jas. 4:6). Christians are commanded to humble themselves under God's mighty hand (1 Pet. 5:6) by utilizing a tool that most Christians use least—the tool of prayer (1 Pet. 5:7). For whatever reason, something as powerful as prayer is utilized inconsistently and/or incorrectly by believers and this is a hindrance to growth.

Nowhere is this more evident than in a small group setting, where unity and maturity could be fostered through prayer, but instead, sharing requests becomes an opportunity for people to air grievances and invite pity. This chapter is designed to make sure that church small groups maximize and exercise the discipline of prayer the way that God intended.

PRAYER AND YOUR SMALL GROUP

One of the major benefits of a small group is the fellowship that can take place through prayer. Sadly, church culture has turned prayer into an individualized activity where one group member asks another to pray, and then nothing more is done. This is not to say that the Bible forbids praying independently of other Christians. In fact, Christ encouraged it (Matt. 6:6) and exemplified it (Mark 1:35), as did others in the Old and New Testaments. Nor should small groups stop informing each other on how they can be praying for one another. However, groups of people praying *together* were a distinct characteristic of the church in the book of Acts (2:42; 12:12), and small groups today should be marked by the same devotion to prayer.

A thriving small group makes a diligent effort to pray together; without this, great dangers face the group. One danger is a temptation to rob God of the glory that he deserves. This means that attention and dependence that should be put on God are eliminated when a group does not pray together. Any good that happens will be seen simply as a "lucky" turn of events, rather than prompt an act of worship because God has answered his people. Credit for growth in the lives of each person will be misapplied if the small group fails to pray together. Lack of prayer will leave glory up for grabs, and unclaimed glory attracts the human heart as light attracts a moth.

Another immediate danger that faces small groups is the misuse of prayer. Small groups have allowed the influence of the personalized, selfish culture to dictate how prayer functions in the group. People's circumstances fill the prayer cards. Members' feelings dominate the prayer time on small group nights. Gossip is tolerated because it comes in the form of a request. This happens because small groups pray from the wrong perspective. To experience the power that prayer offers, each small group member must understand what outlook Christians need to have when they pray.

When circumstances or feelings drive how a small group prays, the group members fall prey to one of Satan's oldest tricks. The devil loves to take what God has made and invert it to bring himself glory. As he did in the garden when he inverted the structure God had given to the family, he has subtly and successfully done the same with prayer. He has deceived Christians into being more concerned with the temporal rather than with the eternal. He has focused believers on the mundane rather than the majestic. By doing so, he has stolen a great weapon in the arsenal of a small group—Bible-saturated, God-glorifying prayer.

Practically speaking, this means that today many small groups pray inaccurately. They have taken how the Lord taught his disciples to pray and inverted it. In Matthew 6:9–15, Jesus demonstrates to his followers that they should pray from the perspective of God's kingdom and his holy name and let that influence how they pray for their daily needs. Instead, people have let daily concerns dominate their prayer lives and now those concerns shape the way they view God, rather than their view of God shaping the way they view their concerns.

It is essential to make sure that prayer is organized and focused. Christ taught a specific way to pray, Paul adopted this pattern in his epistles, and prayer was always done to seek the will of God. Sadly, group prayer can be one of the most unfocused times because people have become enslaved to their circumstances and feelings rather than looking to God for guidance in prayer. This is not to say that providing context for a request is wrong, but it does mean that if you are using small group time to vent about something with no intention of seeking God's will, then there is a problem (John 15:7).

PRAY WITH AN OPEN BIBLE

Often, wants and circumstances instead of God's kingdom, will, and greatness shape small group prayer lists. The temptation to be dominated by prayer requests that have an earthly and finite perspective hinders small group growth and transparency. Christians must get back to using prayer to promote God's agenda and not their own. This will not eliminate the need to ask for practical necessities, but it will put the requests in the right perspective. One should not get the impression that praying for needs is wrong or that the group should only be concerned with deep, theological requests. Instead, prayer for God's kingdom should change the way Christians think about their situations, rather than letting their situations influence how they think about God's kingdom.

Daniel was a great example of using this type of prayer. He was a man who knew the importance and power of prayer, not allowing even the decree of the king to stop him. His supplication recorded in chapter 9 is a prime example of God-glorifying prayer. Daniel confesses sin (v. 5), highlights God's attributes (v. 7, 9), and asks God to ultimately act for his name's sake (v. 19). How was he able to maintain this focus? He prayed with an open Bible (v. 2). If anyone could have let his surroundings take over his time of prayer, Daniel had a pretty good case. But God's word kept his thoughts tethered to the right perspective.

Once group members adopt this practice and idea of prayer, they should not assume that they won't coast back into old habits. How can a small group stay on task in prayer? They need the correct guide when sharing their requests. The remedy for circumstance-driven prayer is Spirit-driven prayer, and the Spirit of God works through the word of God. The disciple of Christ must pray "in the Spirit" (Jude 20), which is not a mystical, emotional, or sentimental state of mind, but a submission to the Spirit's guidance in prayer.

A guide is only as good as his objective knowledge of the area being navigated. In London, a person must train for two to four years to become a cabbie. He spends that time memorizing over 25,000 streets, specific traffic patterns, and 1,400 landmarks in order to be able to pass a test that only three in ten will pass.[20] Why put these people through such rigor? Because the effective cabbie is guided by objective knowledge of the city, not the way he feels might be the best direction to go. So, it is with the Spirit of God, who uses the word of God to navigate believers toward a Christ-like, God-Glorifying focus in prayer.

This idea can be seen in Paul's letter to the Ephesians. In Ephesians 6:17 Paul lists the only offensive weapon used in fighting spiritual battles: It is the "sword of the Spirit which is the word of God." Now, that should be taken as the objective, true, and clear word of God. The next statement should be connected to it, "praying at all times in the Spirit" (v. 18). There is a connection between the Spirit's ability to use the powerful and accurate word of God to lead the believer to powerfully and accurately pray for the will of God. The Spirit only communicates the truth about Christ (1 Cor. 12:1–3; John 16:12–14; 1 John 4:1–2) and when Christians pray according to the revealed will of God in Scripture, they will be directed by the Spirit. Here are two practices that will help a small group stay guided by the Spirit.

Let God Speak First

Before talking through small group questions, it is a good practice to read (or re-read) the passage that was preached in the sermon that will be discussed, and then pray. This gives God the first word in the conversation that the group is going to have with him. After reading the passage, someone (a leader modeling this would be helpful) can pray through the passage, asking God to give insight into the application of his word. Since these small groups are designed to work off of the sermons, and believers are called to be doers of the word (Jas. 1:22–25), a major concern for the group in prayer should be the application of the truth preached. Seeking God for wisdom and knowledge on how to live out this truth will help keep the group focused, as it is led by the Spirit-inspired word.

Paul modeled this when he prayed for the Colossians, that they would be "filled with the knowledge of his will in all spiritual wisdom and understanding, so as to walk in a manner worthy of the Lord fully pleasing to him, bearing good fruit and increasing in the knowledge of God" (1:9–10). Notice that the wisdom and understanding are of the Spirit, and lead to living lives that please God. Small groups that are effective in living out the truth will be small groups that are effective in praying for God to empower them to do so.

Look at God's Resume

Anyone who has gone out looking for employment knows the importance of a resume. People send out resumes to inform companies of who they are and what they can do. And although humans are known to embellish their resumes, God's resume of who he is and what he has done in recorded Scripture is never exaggerated. So, when small group members gather to bring requests before God, they should look at the Bible to embolden and enhance their requests. When sharing their petitions, have each person give a verse that describes an attribute of God or provides a promise that he has given to his people. This practice will keep the focus where it needs to be and will give a greater motivation to pray guided by the Holy Spirit.

Here is how this could help in a modern-day context. Imagine a group member is having a hard time with a boss who is treating him unjustly. Rather than just lamenting to the group and moving on to another person's request, start with a focus on God's justice. Deuteronomy 32:4 says, "The Rock, his work is perfect, for all his ways are justice. A God of faithfulness and without iniquity, just and upright is he." Now the group will have the opportunity to think rightly about this situation and God will get the glory for his work.

This tactic is seen throughout the Psalms as the writer is repeatedly rescued from letting his circumstances shape his outlook on life. The afflicted writer of Psalm 102 is drowning in his temporal circumstances (vv. 1–11), and yet he records a sudden shift in attention from his surrounding enemies to the sovereign, eternal King (v. 12)! He ends by meditating on God's immutability (vv. 25–28). Rather than suffocating in his circumstances, the writer is able to worship. Looking at the resume of who God is will keep groups praying in the right direction—Godward!

THANKSGIVING ALL YEAR ROUND

Every November people anticipate the feast upon which they will gorge on Thanksgiving Day. The holiday is designed to have people focus their attention on what they are thankful for, but it descends quickly back into the gluttonous consumer mentality of "Black Friday" and "Cyber Monday." How does this happen? It is because the idea of thanksgiving has been compartmentalized into a single day rather than an everyday lifestyle. This vital component of thankfulness is also often missing in small group prayer times. Giving thanks will assist in keeping the focus and goal of prayer on God's glory, as well as help the group develop closeness as they watch God at work in each other's lives.

Paul told the Colossians to "Continue steadfastly in prayer, being watchful in it with thanksgiving" (4:2). To pray and not offer thanksgiving reveals the motives of the heart. Like the nine lepers who received healing from Christ but did not return and offer thanks, a group that does not express thanks is only concerned with what they can get from Christ. Any time that a small group spends together offering thanks will be a sanctifying experience.

One practical way to mark this as a characteristic of the group is to have a localized system for the group to express thanks. Whether that is through an email chain or a journal that someone in the group is responsible for, there must be an outlet for people to communicate why, who, or what drives them to thanksgiving. After a system has been established take time during the small group session to share these things and then give thanks to God in prayer!

Leaders, it is important to remember that people learn by imitation. The old saying that "more is caught than taught," is illustrated by the story of a young girl who followed her mom around as she furiously and frustratedly tried to cook and clean for some guests that were coming over for dinner. The mom grumbled and complained as she finished preparations and the little girl listened. Finally, the guests arrived, and it was time to eat. As everyone sat down, the mother (who had been miraculously struck by the politeness fairy) asked her daughter if she wanted to pray for the meal. "I wouldn't know what to say," the little girl replied. "Just say what you hear mommy say to God," said the mother. So, the girl bowed her head and said, "Dear God, why on earth did I invite all these people to dinner?"

It is important to set a correct example of offering thanks to God so that those who are watching will imitate a right understanding of prayer. Jesus gave thanks (Matt. 11:25; John 6:11), and Paul did the same (Eph. 1:3; Phil. 1:3; Col. 1:3), so small group leaders should also be encouraging, and equipping their groups to follow their pattern of thanksgiving.

GET A CHECK UP

While most people agree with the logic and even necessity of regular check-ups for their cars, obstacles like time (and let's face it, money!) keep them from following through. And while that might be okay in the short-term, the painful (and expensive!) long-term effects of not getting routine tune-ups for a car should drive a car owner to get to the mechanic. It would be good for small group leaders to introduce a policy of regular checkups on the group's prayer time to make sure it is working properly.

There are two ways that this can happen. First, have an eye on "the list" to help gauge the spiritual maturity of your group. Take time to look back over some of the prayer emails that have circulated through the group. Is there a noticeable trend toward listing physical aches and pains? How about bad work circumstances? Do people in the group know more about another member's aunt's gall bladder than they do about that member? If there is a severe lack of prayer for God's kingdom and glory, then it would be wise to take some time to talk with the group about the prayer perspective of Jesus. A great piece of advice comes from Pastor Mike Fabarez, who coined the "100-year test."[21] If the request being made will not matter in 100 years, maybe it should be changed to something that will make a lasting difference.

A second way to provide a tune-up for the group's prayer time would be to invite a pastor to the small group for instruction on prayer. The group could ask questions and then be led in a time of prayer by their shepherd. During this time, group members can also get insight into other areas of the church for which they can pray. Having the leadership of a pastor can be a great benefit in diagnosing how the group is utilizing prayer and be very encouraging as the group continues to meet and pray together.

CONCLUSION

Pride has always been a hindrance to God's people and their prayers. In Solomon's day, people were tempted to act arrogantly and not pray, but God graciously reminded them that if they would "humble themselves and pray" he would hear them and act (2 Chron. 7:14). Small groups today are tempted to misuse and abuse prayer pridefully by making it more about their temporary problems than God's eternal program. Once the group members choose to humble themselves and seek God's will in prayer, he will do more than they could imagine (Eph. 3:20).

Chapter 10

CLOSING THE BACK DOOR

How You Can Help People Remain Committed to Church

Hayden Thomas

The concept of retention is widely studied across disciplines. Whether you are running a Fortune-500 company or a mom-and-pop shop, leaders across the globe recognize that there is more to organizational leadership than just attracting people to your organization. Getting people through the front door is daunting enough, but how do you keep them coming back for more? This problem is common enough to boggle the minds of top executives across secular business sectors, but what are the implications for the local church as she embarks on the mission to make disciples who, for one reason or another, aren't sticking around? This issue is widely defined as the "back door problem"—how do we add new souls to our churches and then retain them for maximum discipleship?

I grew up on a small hobby farm in East Texas. Among various other animals, my family owned about 80 head of goats. Occasionally, we would release them from their enclosures to graze on nearby pastures, and every so often, they would escape to other neighboring farms to graze. As good "shepherds," it was our job to track them down and bring them home.

I remember one occasion when our herd was missing from their stables. When my grandfather and I found them wandering in the neighboring fields, we guided them back safely into their enclosure through the front gate. Feeling satisfied, we returned to the house and sat on the front porch, sipping sweet tea and listening to Paul Harvey on the radio. After several hours, we glanced over into the herd's enclosure to see the goats escaping, one by one, through a small opening in the back of the fence. All the time and effort we spent earlier that day gathering them back through the front gate was of no value once they discovered the opening that we missed…and out they went for "greener pastures," when everything they needed was already right in front of them.

We knew the hole had to be fixed before spending another few hours returning the goats to their enclosure and showing them that everything they could desire was already there. This is a similar picture to many of our churches today. We toil tirelessly to invite souls to join us, to sit under the teaching of God's word, and to the fellowship of the saints, only to lose out on the opportunity for further discipleship because they find a way out through unknown holes in the church's infrastructure. Your church may have everything necessary for healthy discipleship, but without proper direction and oversight, many people will leave believing they must go somewhere else to find what they need.

This chapter is dedicated to the endeavor of closing the back doors of our churches for maximum discipleship. As you have discovered in the previous chapters of this book, the most effective means of discipleship in your church is sermon-based small groups. But what if I told you that sermon-based small groups are also the answer to closing the back door of your church? In the following pages, I will identify five ways sermon-based small groups close the back door, *and how you can implement them.*

THE PATHWAY TO COMMUNITY IS SIMPLIFIED

Have you ever gone to the supermarket with one item on your list, spent 30 minutes wandering the aisles, and then left with a dozen things you didn't need? You arrive home and empty the bags just to realize you forgot the one item you drove to the market for in the first place. How frustrating!

Unfortunately, this is the case with many searching for a home church. A new family arrives at the church's worship service looking for community. By the time they leave the service, they have a bulletin, a kid's craft, a doughnut, a new guest t-shirt, and a car full of hungry kiddos. But were they given the opportunity to connect with your church beyond that Sunday? They left without the one thing they needed most—community.

Sermon-based small groups simplify the age-old question, "How do you get connected with your church?" When new guests arrive at your church looking for community they should hear from the stage, from the church members who greet them, and from the connect team they meet after the service, that the best way to find community is to join a small group.

This all-in approach to sermon-based small groups keeps everyone within your church on the same page, including those who are visiting. New guests also benefit from being fully equipped to jump into a small group immediately that week. They already heard the curriculum preached, and have the sermon application questions in hand, so all that is left for them to do is to find a group and jump in!

Finding a small group should be just as easy. If almost every person the guest encounters is active in a small group, a simple inquiry from them, or an invitation by a church member will assimilate the guest into a small group. This is where you come in! Each Sunday is an opportunity for you to close the back door of your church. Every soul who enters the front doors is a soul who needs community. You are the connecting point between a guest and your group. Much like Philip in John 1:43–46, your job as a growing disciple is to invite others to come and see who Jesus is. Ultimately, your role is to invite others along the discipleship journey with you. The best way to accomplish this is to invite new guests to your small group so they can see disciples living together for the Kingdom of God. This simple but powerful commitment to sermon-based small groups provides an easy pathway for everyone to find a place, thus closing the back door of your church.

EVERYONE IS KNOWN AND LED

Pastorally speaking, knowing who is a member of your church by attending regularly, serving, and giving is of biblical importance. As a matter of fact, 1 Peter 5:2 commands pastors to shepherd the flock of God among them, exercising oversight. This text demands an accounting of both who is a member and how each member is being cared for spiritually. Although there are many ways for pastors to know and lead their church practically, there is no more effective way to accomplish the knowing and leading of members than church-wide, sermon-based small groups.

On the farm, there is a benefit in taking large numbers and making smaller groups. This simple technique provides for more specific care and nurture of the herd. It also allows for closer inspection of the herd and a more equitable balance of resources. Church small groups will accomplish the equitable and individual care necessary in the life of a healthy church.

The shepherds equip the deacons/ministry leaders to divide up a large number of souls under their care. The deacons/ministry leaders serving under the guidance of their pastors can tend to individual needs and focus on discipleship at the micro-level. Furthermore, when the need for greater pastoral care and counseling arises in an individual's life, the small group model allows for easy access to the pastors who already know the small group leaders and hopefully, most of the members of the small groups.

The sermon-based aspect of small groups is one key to effectively leading each small group. Instead of every group choosing a different curriculum or being inspired by whatever subject comes to mind that week, the pastor's message from the previous weekend provides the curriculum and direction for the small group. This structured approach allows pastors to accomplish what God has called them to do—lead. Each small group is taken verse-by-verse through the Bible by the Holy

Spirit's guidance and the pastor's commitment to expository preaching. And, if the pastor is doing his job well, the sermon and the application questions will provide a contextual fit unlike anything else a small group could study that week.

As a church member, you factor into this equation in at least three ways. First, ensure you are connected to a small group so that you are being shepherded. God calls you and everyone else, including your pastors, to live under the church's leadership. No one is an exception to this command.

Second, every soul in a small group should work both to invite people to weekend services and increase the number of new people in their church's small group ministry who can benefit from the church leadership. Church growth without a strong small group ministry is not sustainable over the long term. Therefore, as a major discipleship strategy of a healthy church, small group ministries should always be recruiting new guests into their groups. A 2023 statistic shows that 54% of churches are in decline, only 12% are stable, and 33% are growing.[22] You can be sure that your church is in decline when small group ministries stop growing. Equally valid, however, is that when small groups are growing, your church is growing. If your church is growing, that means you should work hard to ensure everyone is plugged into a small group so they can be known and led.

Lastly, with all the small group growth your church is experiencing, your church needs more small group leaders. Whether you are a new or seasoned Christian, you should pray and consider how God might use you in small group leadership in the future. Although not everyone is called to small group leadership, everyone must pray and consider how God would use them to create a healthy and robust small group ministry in their church.

When you think about closing the back door to your church, nothing can close the door better than a congregation committed to growing healthy small groups that know their pastors and follow their lead.

EVERYONE IS CONNECTED TO THE OVERALL MISSION OF THE CHURCH

Have you ever attended a church where each ministry had a different mission statement? I know a church where every ministry seemed to have a purpose and direction distinct from that of the whole church. What made this even worse was that most church members could not tell you the mission of the ministry they were involved in, or the church's mission posted on the church website. This compartmentalization of ministry and mission leads to a lot of confusion as church members are pulled in different directions and guests are perplexed at which direction they should go to connect to the community.

Again, this is where sermon-based small groups come in. When there is a commitment for every soul in your church to join a sermon-based small group, the homogeneity created is difficult to find in any other organizational structure. Instead of ministries going in all different directions with a limited resource pool, everyone is playing from the same playbook and going in the same direction. Each ministry will likely have its distinct demographical makeup, but their connection is inextricably linked through sermon-based small groups.

You may be asking, what about singles ministry, or men's and women's ministry? What if I told you that you can have all those ministries in alignment with the church's overall mission by using sermon-based small groups? As your ministries meet, the same emphasis is on the weekend sermon but with specific application for men, women, and singles. At my church, we go one step further; our men's and women's ministries meet once a month, and when they break into small groups, the men and women break into the same small group that they belong to during the weeknights. This interconnectedness has proven to grow interpersonal intimacy, and a commitment to the overall mission and vision of the church corporately. On top of that, when new men and women visit our once-a-month events, we can point them to sermon-based small groups immediately, thus accomplishing the overall vision of our church.

I get it. This kind of commitment may not be the front door to your church that you envisioned. But your commitment to the overarching mission and vision of church-wide sermon-based small groups is one of the best ways to close the back door and ensure that your church truly has a place for everyone.

ACCOUNTABILITY AND ENCOURAGEMENT ARE BUILT-IN

There seems to be a never-ending barrage of affinity groups—Life Groups, Discipleship Groups, Accountability Groups, Recovery Groups, Fellowship Groups, etc. within our churches today. I am not against affinity groups; many serve the Lord well in their respective areas. However, I cannot help but think of the disservice that can come from compartmentalizing the "one another" passages in the New Testament to different groups within the church. For example, Romans 15:14 teaches us to *admonish* one another, this Greek word *noutheteō*, is often used in the context of biblical counseling. But what if we reserved this command for only the pastoral staff or certain affinity groups, meeting at different times throughout the week, tasked with the command to counsel? This ministry philosophy would require different groups for every felt need in the disciple's life.

Another example is found in James 5:16, which teaches us to confess our sins to one another. What if we needed to join a specific accountability group before we exercised this command? Limiting each group to a specific felt need hinders the fullness of life-on-life ministry that we see in the New Testament community. Sermon-based small groups can be the most effective means for the communal fulfillment of all the "one another" passages in Scripture.

Done correctly, a sermon-based small group is a catalyst for ongoing community throughout life. The same people you meet with weekly for sermon application questions are those you break bread with on other nights during the week. The same men or women you meet with each week in your small group are the same men and women you meet with during men's and women's fellowships. When the time for encouragement and accountability is needed, which is regularly, you have these one another's built into the fabric of your life through your small group.

What does this have to do with closing the back door? Suppose you can show people that they do not need to search far and wide for accountability, encouragement, assistance, or a host of other felt needs.

It goes a long way toward closing the back door of your church when people find that their needs can be met within the structure of your church.

A CLOSED BACK DOOR, BUT NOT A LOCKED BACK DOOR

I hope you desire for your church to grow, as dying and plateauing churches are not God's desire. His will is for vibrant church communities that fulfill the "one another's." An integral key to a growing church is retaining those who come through the front doors. We want to ensure that we do everything possible to invite, connect, and engage with people about the gospel, then invite them into the biblical community by assimilating them into the church family. This does require strategic thinking and strong organizational leadership. But as much as we want to close the back door to prevent people from leaving the church prematurely, we do not want to lock the back door, making it impossible for anyone to leave, who may have good reasons for doing so.

Therefore, we must understand that closing the back door to our churches is not caging our congregations, but fencing the perimeters of doctrine, fellowship, and discipleship. This kind of fencing is essential to healthy ecclesiology. What is a church? The answer to this question necessitates structural boundaries and commitments between the leaders and the congregants. But these structures do not include locking the back door and throwing away the key. This may be the pattern of cults, but it is not the pattern of the true Church.

There are several instances when members are faced with the need to find another local church: when families move, when new churches are planted, and when there are irreconcilable convictions between leadership and individuals. In these instances, I am convinced that we can open the back door, and a God-honoring, Christ-exalting, orderly transition can occur. It is a transition where those who leave are known, counseled, and sent out with full knowledge and transparency. I am not suggesting a clandestine operation where we slip people out of the back of our church. Instead, we can acknowledge a use for the back door that provides a safe and healthy outlet for church transition. But in my estimation, those are the only reasons we want to open the back door.

A back door suggests a limited opportunity for exiting the life of the church, which is precisely what a healthy church should desire. For members of the church, this is helpful as well. Instead of wondering, who has left the church? Do the pastors know? Should I say something? You can simply inquire whether the individuals you are thinking of have exited in an orderly and appropriate way through the backdoor. If not, that is the perfect opportunity to reach out to those individuals to bring them back into the fold.

CONCLUSION

When my wife and I host gatherings at our home, we do our best to direct everyone to the rooms and resources they need to be familiar with to have a comfortable and lasting visit. We inform them where the restroom and sitting areas are located and even direct them away from rooms that may be unnecessary for their stay. We hope this kind of orientation to our home keeps our guests from wandering around guessing what room will meet their needs. I would hate to watch them accidentally walk out the back door of my home, looking for something they could have found if I were a better host.

This same concept is valid in the church. We never want to assume guests know where to go and how to get connected to community. Just because someone walks through the front door does not mean they know where their next steps will lead them. Many who visit your church may wander around until they stumble upon the backdoor and walk out, assuming, since they did not find what they were looking for on their own, that the search for community must go on elsewhere. That's why closing the back door takes a carefully organized process that ensures pastors and members can account for every soul who enters the front doors of your church. Of course, this does not promise that every person who walks through the front door will stay, but it does assure that everyone who desires genuine community will always have the opportunity to find it.

Sermon-based small groups provide an easy onramp to the church's communal life and are a simplified structure that exists to meet the needs of every soul at the church. Implemented well, the back door is utilized in limited cases that arise and is mostly forgotten by the majority of souls who have found a church home in your congregation.

Chapter 11

SMALL SMALL GROUPS

Why Keep Small Groups "Small"?

Lucas Pace

When a church grows numerically you can count on its small groups growing in size. As disciples are made, they will seek to connect with other brothers and sisters in Christ, and not only will the existing small groups expand in size, but new small groups will need to be established. In time, for many groups, the title of "*small* group" will no longer be applicable.

On the one hand, "large groups" are a reason to praise the Lord because souls have been saved, discipleship is happening, and new believers are seeking to get connected to fellow Christians. However, it can become problematic if the size of the "small groups" becomes detrimental to their intended purpose of seeing Christians connect to deepen their relationships with God and others through discussion of Scripture, accountability, and fellowship. So, let's consider how to handle this "good problem" of small groups growing too large for their own good.

WHY SMALL GROUPS AND NOT LARGE GROUPS

Imagine the perfect small group. You would likely picture a leader or two who are highly invested in their group. The group would comfortably fill a living room and the people would know each other, care about one another, and enjoy spending time with each other. Meaningful conversations would be taking place, and after each group meeting people would leave with just what they needed—whether they were encouraged, challenged, loved, or admonished. The participants would drive home being more faithful doers of God's word, because of the time they had spent together as a group.

This type of group does not "just happen." It requires trained, caring, and godly leaders, as well as small group members who want to get the most out of their time with their small group. And, as I have said, it also requires that the small group is not too big. A group should not be so large that there is not enough time for every member to add to the discussion during each meeting. It should never grow so big that the members hardly know each other, and the leaders don't have enough time to fully invest in those who are under their care. A group should not have so many participants that when you share personal information, you might as well post it on the internet. It shouldn't get to the size that it goes unnoticed when someone is missing or needs extra care. There comes a time when a small group gets too big and loses the ability to be effective. Let's look further into the key reasons we need to make sure our small groups stay small.

Absentees Should be Missed

In the early church, it is doubtful that the Apostles knew whether "Fred and Wilma" were part of the three thousand-plus disciples that showed up for the teaching in the temple courtyard every day. Much less if they were actually applying what they were learning from the teaching of God's word. When those three thousand-plus believers connected with one another it would take place in each other's homes (Acts 5:42) which, as we saw in the first chapter, is very similar to modern-day small groups. Fred and Wilma would have been identified or easily noticed as being absent from one of these smaller house gatherings.

In larger churches today, people can go unnoticed and are not missed if they don't show up for church on the weekend. That is why small groups are necessary—we need to care for people and lovingly pursue them when they don't show up. Their presence and participation should be expected in their small group meeting. As groups grow in size, it becomes more of a challenge to ensure everyone is adding to the conversation and not being overlooked. Eventually, there can be so many people in the "small group" that if Fred and Wilma do not show up, their lack of attendance is not felt, noted, or responded to.

Everyone Should be Known

The purpose of a small group is to get beneath surface conversations and care about what is "really" going on in each other's lives. Big gatherings are like a neighborhood block party which only allows for shallow relationships. Instead of a block party, small groups should have an intimate atmosphere that lends itself to better opportunities for "real" connections, similar to inviting another family over for a sit-down meal. Of course, a smaller group does not guarantee personal and transparent conversations, but it does make it more possible and more inviting. A group that is the size of a large family, rather than a small church, provides the opportunity for Christians to be vulnerable and let their guard down.

Speaking of family, as we go deeper in conversation and see the real needs in each other's lives, we can meet those needs as a family would. However, when a group is too large it is not conducive to members going deeper and sharing their struggles, or a need for encouragement. There may be too many faces to notice those who are hurting. In large groups, people can slip through the cracks or go unnoticed when they most need their spiritual brothers and sisters supporting, challenging, or helping them. However, if this "family feel" is created, people will be truly known, and the needs of the church can be met through the small groups. Engaging in relationships through deeper conversations has far more benefits than mere honesty. It allows us to know the needs of our brothers and sisters in Christ and meet the needs as God commands us to (1 John 3:16–18; Jas. 2:15–16).

Group Time Should Not Take All Night

I have visited other countries where church members meet in each other's homes until the late hours of the night, and even into the early morning hours of the next day. As I was struggling to keep my eyes open, people were conversing and digging deeper into one another's lives. Different cultures have different expectations. People in our Western culture, generally speaking, are not expecting nor conditioned to benefit from a six-hour small group meeting. We are a time-sensitive culture, where people and activities operate with an expected starting time and ending time, usually not more than a couple of hours.

The size of a small group and the amount of time allotted for the meeting will affect the ability to dig deeper into each other's lives, as well as impact participation. The bigger the group, the more time it will take to accomplish our goals. We can expect people to be looking at their watches and checking out of the conversation as time drags on too long because everyone in the not-so-small group is sharing and going deeper. Simple math would tell us that every person we add to the group should have some time to share in the discussion, thus each person adds several minutes to the meeting time. There comes a point when we are either losing quality participation or our meeting time is just too long.

A Leader Should be Involved in Participants' Lives

The number of small group participants also plays a determining factor in how effective the leaders can be in caring for those in their group. A leader's job does not begin when the small group meeting starts, nor does it conclude when the meeting ends. Much of the leader's job takes place outside of the small group meeting.

As a father of six children, I have to manage my schedule carefully to be able to spend quality time with each of my children and not end up an absentee dad. I don't think I would be able to be the kind of father I desire to be if I had fifteen children. Not only would I not be the Dad I would want to be, but I would also not be able to faithfully fulfill my role as a husband, nor complete my responsibilities at work and in ministry. Likewise, small group leaders should not have so many members to care for that they can't keep up with investing in each person and continue to faithfully tackle their role in their biological families, jobs, as well as other responsibilities.

As the small group grows, the leader will have to set aside additional time outside of the meeting to invest and follow up with those who are in their small group. Obviously, a time will come when there are too many people for the leader to continue to be effective at caring for each person in the group.

Large groups can easily make it more difficult for groups to be effective. Strategically small small groups will promote one hundred percent participation, enable digging deeper into each other's lives, and also present the opportunity for the leader to invest in each participant outside of the meeting time. However, in a thriving church, small groups are going to grow. So, what do we do to prevent our small group from becoming a large group?

Identify and Train Your Replacement

When the church grows you will need more small groups and small group leaders, and new leaders are best produced from existing small groups. Some might wonder why brand-new groups are not just formed with all new people. There are several reasons this may not be the most effective route.

First, consider the training of new leaders. Those who are in a small group have personally seen how small groups work, they have already proved to be faithful and mature participants of a small group and are positioned to replicate the success they have seen and experienced in their own group.

Second, think about the benefits to new members. There is a great advantage in bringing new people into an already established group that has momentum in applying God's word. New church members can join an established group and rise to the maturity level of the group. Established groups will also be full of well-connected individuals who can rightly help new people by getting them connected and involved at the church.

Also, those who have been a part of a church and small group for a while should have increased knowledge, experience, and maturity, which new small group members, and brand-new Christians, could benefit from greatly. Those mature believers should be a part of every group, rather than having new groups formed that only include new churchgoers and new believers.

Lastly, it is beneficial to establish a church culture that encourages others to join established small groups rather than leave newcomers with the sense that groups are "closed" or "exclusive." So, in most cases, it is best to launch small groups from within small groups that are already growing. This requires existing leaders to see their small group as a developmental league for training new leaders.

Sure, not every small group participant is going to become a small group leader, but often a group includes those who can and should be. Unfortunately, far too often those with the potential to lead are never identified and trained to do so. These "could be" leaders are far less productive in ministry because no one identifies them, seeks them out, and challenges them to take their role in a small group to the next level.

Identify Potential Small Group Leaders

I think about my death often. I am not depressed or dreary but am trying to be responsible. I want my house in order if I die, ensuring my family will be cared for (life insurance helps). I also want my ministry in order, by having someone able and ready to take my place. I know that God is the one who will ultimately take care of my family and provide a qualified person to carry on my ministry post, however, I think it is a biblical pattern to have an understudy who is ready to take over your position and even expand the ministry while you are still living. Moses had Joshua, Eli had Samuel, Elijah had Elisha, Jesus had the twelve and focused largely on three—Peter, John, and James. Barnabas had Paul and Mark, and Paul had Timothy, Titus, Luke, and others. Who do you have? Have you identified the next person God may have lead a small group, or take over your small group so you can start a new one? Or maybe God wants to move you so you can serve in a different ministry. Have you found your replacement?

What are you looking for in a future small group leader? We could generate a list of attributes and characteristics that would make for the ideal leader, but one general, yet essential quality to look for is faithfulness. As Paul tells Timothy, "I thank him who has given me strength, Christ Jesus our Lord, because he judged me *faithful*, appointing me to his service" (1 Tim. 1:12 emphasis added). In "sermon-based" small groups, leaders are not required to teach (which is a qualification for pastors, 1 Tim. 3), but they must be faithful in a very broad sense.

Potential leaders need to be faithful to God's Word, both in obedience and doctrinal soundness. They need to be faithful in attendance at church and consistently show up for their small group. They need to faithfully participate in the discussions and show they are pointing the discussion back to the Bible. They need to show that they can facilitate a conversation about the "application questions" (CBC sermon-based small groups are based on application questions that the preacher writes) and not reteach the sermon or teach something new (using small groups as a platform to promote their own agenda). They must be faithful and submissive to the pastoral oversight of those who would be entrusting to them a position of leadership. You should be looking for someone dependable, reliable, and most of all faithful in these categories.

Train Future Small Group Leaders

Numerous books have been written on training leaders. This section is not intended to provide intensive material on how to train new leaders (most churches will have additional material to train and equip leaders), but rather is intended as a reminder of a few essential components that are foundational to developing new leaders.

Model what to do. As Paul told Timothy "Follow the pattern of the sound words that you have heard from me, in the faith and love that are in Christ Jesus." (2 Tim. 1:13). You should set an example of what a faithful small group leader looks like. During every small group meeting, how you lead is being observed. Group members will notice how you draw people into the conversation, how you firmly redirect those who speak too much, how you bring rabbit trails back to the intended topic, how you dig beneath surface-level answers to bring application to every person, how you settle controversial and heated conversations, and many other things. Remember you are being watched!

It is important to be transparent with a potential leader regarding all the things that you do throughout the week that go unnoticed by many: meeting up for coffee with someone in the group who is struggling and needs accountability, texting those who need encouragement, the amount of time you spend in prayer and prep for each small group meeting, etc. Provided that you are a good leader, you should want the potential leader to imitate you in every way (1 Cor. 4:16–17).

You also need to step back to let someone step up. After Timothy spent time observing Paul, Paul gave him ministry work to do (1 Cor. 16:10). There are plenty of opportunities and jobs that you can entrust to a potential leader. One such opportunity is to have your understudy lead the prayer time in your group, or you might suddenly, yet purposefully, be unable to attend the small group meeting one night, so the potential leader will *have* to step up and lead. As a leader, you should not hold on to all the responsibilities, because doing so will prevent someone else from growing and becoming a leader.

Prayer is essential in every aspect of the Christian life. As a leader you need to pray for the next leader, as he or she will have lots of obstacles to overcome in stepping up to lead—prayer is crucial. There is no doubt that Satan has an agenda to take leaders down and out, especially those who are in the beginning stages of leadership (Luke 22:31). Thus, Jesus prayed for Peter (Luke 22:32) who would be the upcoming leader of the church. Paul constantly prayed for Timothy (2 Tim. 1:3) and reminded him to be the leader that God had called him to be (1 Tim. 1:5–7). You too need to develop a regular habit of specifically praying and encouraging those potential leaders in your group.

Moving From One to Two Groups

So, the church is growing, your small group is bordering on being a "large group," and your understudy is ready to lead (with the approval of the pastoral leadership) ... it is time to split into two groups! You can avoid the drama of "blowing up" your small group by always reminding each member of Jesus' command to make disciples and communicating the vision of the church in seeing those disciples connected to one another. It is understandable, and even a good thing, that the members of the group like the group as it is and don't desire massive change. It would be unfortunate if they hoped the group would split up! However, the priority of seeing more people saved and connected in the church should override the comfort of the current familiar small group. In time, groups with new members or new leaders may change a little, but each group should always be a place where members grow, are challenged, and connect in meaningful relationships with other brothers and sisters in Christ.

You will want to be strategic in how your group expands into two groups. Is the new leader going to start leading the current group so the old leader can start a new one? Is the new leader going to start a new group and bring several other people from the current group along? There is no one way to do it! However, it is important to communicate what is going on and why there is a need to create another group to your current group—so that every member of the group can praise God that more people are being connected in the church. This news should also motivate all the members to pray that the new group will accomplish the objective of getting people connected in order to deepen relationships with God and others through discussion of Scripture, accountability, and fellowship.

CONCLUSION

While a large "small group" is a problem, it is certainly a good problem to have. How great would it be if your church was growing so rapidly by adding new disciples who wanted to get connected, that new small groups needed to be created? We should be thankful when groups need to split off to create new groups so that everyone can get plugged into an effective "small group." Let's pray that this need does arise and that current leaders will wisely navigate their groups to better help people connect to each other and apply God's word to their lives.

NOTES

[1] The following material is adapted from my workbook, Mike Fabarez, *Partners: One-on-One Discipleship* (Aliso Viejo, CA: Focal Point Ministries, 2020), 143–155.

[2] Brooke Still, "Ten Ways Food Waste Hurts the Environment," April 10, 2017, https://www.feedingamerica.org/hunger-blog/ten-ways-food-waste-hurts-the-environment.

[3] "Hunger in America," https://www.feedingamerica.org/hunger-in-america.

[4] John A. Broadus, *A Treatise on the Preparation and Delivery of Sermons*, New Edition, ed. Edwin C. Dargan (New York: Hodder & Stoughton, 1898), 245.

[5] Robert D. Putnam, *Bowling Alone: The Collapse and Revival of American Community* (New York: Simon & Schuster, 2000).

[6] I want to insert a special thanks to the Compass Bible Institute students who took my course, Small Groups and Discipleship, and read early versions of this chapter and others in this book. Their insightful class interaction and feedback, which stemmed from real experiences in small
group settings, helped shape my understanding of small group ministry and improve this book as a whole.

[7] Small group leaders need to recognize that part of their job in leading a group is shepherding people within the group, and this is inevitably going to involve confrontation with sin. This does not require that you carry a whistle and blast

people for their sin all the time, but it does mean you should feel the weight of responsibility to lead people spiritually. And, when necessary, you rise up to carefully and gently restore those who need to be helped out of their sin.

[8] Depending on the group and the problem, it may very well be the best thing to devote the entire session to the individual. Wisdom is essential here.

[9] C. W. Ellison, "Trust," in *Baker Encyclopedia of Psychology & Counseling*, eds. David G. Benner and Peter C. Hill (Grand Rapids: Baker Books, 1999), 1232.

[10] Tim Challies, "How to Make Accountability Work," January 20, 2014, http://www.challies.com/articles/how-to-make-accountability-work; adapted from Heath Lambert, *Finally Free* (Grand Rapids: Zondervan, 2013), 45–57.

[11] Gerhard Kittel, ed. *Theological Dictionary of the New Testament*, trans. G. W. Bromily, vol. 5 (Grand Rapids: Eerdmans, 1976), 151.

[12] Evan Andrews, "How Patrick Henry's 'Liberty of Death' Speech Inspired Revolution," August 23, 2023, https://www.history.com/news/patrick-henrys-liberty-or-death-speech-240-years-ago.

[13] C. S. Lewis, *Mere Christianity* (New York: HarperCollins Publishers, 2001), 56–57.

[14] "President Dan Cathy Talks about Chic-fil-A's Unusual Keys to Success," March 21, 2012, http://www.tampabay.com/news/business/retail/president-dan-cathy-talks-about-chick-fil-as-unusual-keys-to-success/1221191.

[15] Jonathan Edwards, *Jonathan Edwards' Resolutions and Advice to Young Converts*, ed. Stephen J. Nichols (Phillipsburg, NJ: P&R Publishing, 2001), 20.

[16] Ian H. Murray, "Robert Murray M'Cheyne," November 12, 2001, https://banneroftruth.org/us/resources/articles/2001/robert-murray-mcheyne/.

[17] Mike Fabarez, *Partners: One-on-One Discipleship* (Aliso Viejo, CA: Focal Point Ministries, 2020), 119.

[18] Much of this material was originally gleaned from a now out-of-print book, Allen Hadidian *Successful Discipling* (Chicago: Moody Press, 1979).

[19] Original source unknown.

[20] Joshua Foer, *Moonwalking with Einstein: The Art and Science of Remembering Everything* (New York: Penguin Books, 2012), 38.

[21] Mike Fabarez, "Israel's Greatest Hits: Vol. II, Part 4" (Compass Bible Church sermon, Aliso Viejo, CA, March 31, 2019), https://focalpointministries.org/product/israels-greatest-hits-vol-ii-part-4/.

[22] "Back to Normal? The Mixed Messages of Congregational Recovery Coming Out of the Pandemic," August 2023, https://www.covidreligionresearch.org/wp-content/uploads/2023/09/Epic-4-2.pdf.

COMPASS BIBLE CHURCH

Compass Bible Church was planted in Orange County, California in 2005, and is committed to reaching people for Christ, teaching people to be like Christ, and training people to serve Christ.

Learn more at www.compasschurch.org

COMPASS BIBLE INSTITUTE

Compass Bible Institute, founded by Pastor Mike Fabarez and Compass Bible Church Aliso Viejo, provides thorough biblical education and hands-on training to prepare individuals for leadership in Christian ministry. CBI offers full degrees, certificates, and graduate level courses with credits transferring to partnering colleges, universities, and seminaries.

compassbibleinstitute.org/

FOCAL POINT MINISTRIES

Focal Point Radio Ministries is the Bible teaching ministry of Dr. Mike Fabarez. Since 1998 Focal Point has been proclaiming the depths of Scripture on the radio, online, and in print. Focal Point can be heard on over 800 outlets across the United States. Access to the radio program, sermons and devotionals is also available through the Focal Point App.

focalpointministries.org/

CCPA — COMPASS CHURCH PLANTING ASSOCIATION

The Compass Church Planting Association is an association of churches committed to working hard at replicating more churches that highlight and promote the expository preaching of God's word.

focalpointministries.org/

NEC — NATIONAL EQUIPPED CONFERENCE

The National Equipped Conference is designed to provide Christians with biblical instruction and practical motivation to effectively live the Christian life and fruitfully serve God's Church. The NEC is a biennial event, hosted by the Compass Church Planting Association.

equippedconference.com/